TURNING YOUR PASSION
INTO YOUR PROFESSION

TODAY

by

BILLY HORTON

Published by RICHER Press
An Imprint of Richer Life, LLC

5710 Ogeechee Road, Suite 200-175, Savannah, Georgia 31405
www.richerlifellc.com

Volume book discounts are available for groups, companies and organizations. Contact the publisher for information.

TODAY
Turning Your Passion Into Your Profession

Billy Horton

1. Self-Help   2. Inspiration 3. Educational
[pbk : alk. Paper]

Print Book: ISBN-13: 979-8-9863598-7-8

PRINTED IN THE UNITED STATES OF AMERICA

March 2025

DEDICATION

This book is dedicated to everyone who has the courage to step out in faith and pursue the dream that God has put in their heart.

ACKNOWLEDGEMENTS

I have grown into the man, husband, and father that I am today because of the people that God has put into my life. I am forever thankful to all of you.

Taleen, my beautiful wife who puts up with my shenanigans. I know I drive you crazy, but you said yes at the alter and now you are stuck with me.

Connor and Bryce, my two amazing sons. I swell with pride when I look at you and thank the Lord for giving me the opportunity to be your dad. I love you both very much.

Momma Horton for being my biggest fan since I picked up a bat. Your support and generosity will always be near and dear to my heart.

Bill Crawford and Mike Stanley for being the sages that I so dearly need for wisdom.

My advisory team that acts as my sounding board and help hold me accountable: Andre Wadsworth, Chris Sylvester, Danny Putnam, Jim Reid, Jon Huizinga, Kory DeHaan, and Steve Stanley. I am extremely blessed to also call you my friends.

Travis Hearn, Todd Boffo, and all the men in our bible study at Impact Church. You have sharpened, challenged, and loved me just like a brother.

The men who wrote endorsements for this book. Your encouraging words gave me confidence that this will make a big impact in people's lives.

Rusty the All-American redbone coonhound. You are my walking buddy, security guard and loyal companion.

Finally, all the people who put in the hard work getting this book completed and on the shelf. Earl Cobb and the publishing team at RICHER Press, and Erica Smith for her diligent work getting the cover art done for this book. All of you are responsible for helping make this a reality and I am so thankful for all the hours you put in.

ENDORSEMENTS

"In life we all search for purpose and a sense of belonging. We embark on many journeys only to come up empty. Sometimes we need a little help along the way, God's hand leading us, someone's testimony, or even a cheat sheet. If that sounds like you then you've picked up the right book."

Howie Kendrick
Special Assistant to the General Manager of the Philadelphia Phillies and former 15-year Major League Veteran Infielder

"Billy has done an amazing job laying out practical steps on how to pursue the passions that God has given you. His life story, intertwined with ups and downs, will encourage you in so many ways. Keep learning and praying and pursuing your passions for helping people, and you will be right where God wants you to be."

Kory DeHaan
Co-Owner of HitLab Palmetto, former Major League Outfielder, and 12-year Minor League Coach

"You can't help but feel Billy's passion as you read this book. I had a smile on my face while reading because I have been a witness to watching God direct his steps as he stepped out in faith! Let his words inspire you to action in your own life."

Steve Stanley
Owner of the Stanley Agency and former Minor League & Two-Time NCAA All-American Outfielder

"It might be too soon to call this book a classic, but if correctly applied, Billy Horton's message can be used to be successful in anything you put your mind and effort to. But most importantly, to impact human lives for the Kingdom of God."

Bobby Magallanes
Major League Assistant Hitting Coach for the Seattle Mariners and former Minor League Infielder

"Billy's story reminds all of us to lean upon the Lord as we seek His calling and direction for our lives."

Bobby Evans
Special Advisor to the President of Baseball Operations for the San Francisco Giants and Former Major League General Manager

"Stuck living in the past? Worrying about the future? By reading TODAY, Billy Horton provides actionable processes to take a hold of your life and live it in a more Godly way."

Tyler LaTorre
Head Baseball Coach Pepperdine University, 2023 NAIA National Coach of the Year, and former Minor League Catcher

"Leveraging a simple acronym, Billy delivers a powerful tool enabling both personal growth and leadership development. His conversational tone and humility allow for an easy read rooted in credibility and universal applicability. Whether new to the work force or a seasoned career professional, TODAY offers a framework that helps align passion, purpose, and potential."

Christopher Sylvester
Commander, United States Navy (Retired) 24-year Military Veteran

TABLE OF CONTENTS

Dedication   iii

Acknowledgements   v

Endorsements   vii

Introduction   11

Take Action   15

Overcome   27

Dream   41

Achieve   55

Yes   69

The Setback   85

The Comeback   101

Epilogue   119

Glossary of Verses   121

About the Author   125

Photographs - *Baseball and Family Memories*   127

INTRODUCTION

Many things happen on our journey into a career choice. Life is a series of experiences that help define who we are and who we will become. Along the way we make decisions and determine if the risk involved is worth the reward in the end. I believe we are all called to live amazing lives that will bless others. It takes a balance of wisdom and courage to follow our passions into our profession.

Some people know what they want to do seemingly from birth. Their grandfather was a fireman, their dad is a fireman, and all they can ever think about is the opportunity to jump on Engine #9 as soon as humanly possible. Others may be born into the family business and look forward to the time when the responsibility falls on them to carry on the tradition. Some have no idea what they want to do for a career and search for it as they would hidden treasure.

There are those of us take who take our high school and college years to figure out our career path. It is a time of experimentation. We try different things and take classes that interest us. The thought of picking a major our freshman year of college seems too stressful, so we take some core classes that work towards any major that the university offers. Upon graduation we may even decide to go a different route and get a job that does not even match the education that we invested so much money in.

I believe that deep down many of us want to make a significant impact on the lives of others and be a world changer. We want to make a difference, and our heart is to help others. The vision is there, but we may become afraid that the summit will be too hard to climb. The worry of what might happen takes us to a place of fear and we quit before we start. There are also those who have no idea what they want to do and wander aimlessly hoping that their destiny will somehow find them.

Choosing a career also comes at different times in people's lives. From little kids dreaming, to high school and college graduates setting lofty goals, to someone making a change when they are in their thirties or forties, you can't put a date on when decisions about your profession will be made in your lifetime. Hopefully you have someone that can give you wisdom and you can lean on when times like this surface. It is important to have people who can speak into your life and deeply care about your future.

On this journey I believe many of us come to a fork in the road when deciding on what to do for a career. For some the fork has to do with how much money they are going to be able to make. Others are more concerned about being happy in their job and money is not the focus. I believe that we all want to have a profession where we love our job and are compensated well for doing it while impacting the lives of others in a positive way.

I am here to tell you that it is possible for all of us, and that the road is not always paved. At least for me, it wasn't. Years ago, I decided to write down every company that I have received a paycheck from since I was sixteen years old, and I kept updating the list. They are all written on a seven-inch piece of register tape that you would find in most ten key calculators.

The total amount, front and back, was 48. Forty-Eight!!! Of these jobs I was fired or released from my contract a staggering nine times. The numbers shocked me and after letting them sink in I became so thankful for how God always provided for me.

It wasn't until March 2006 when I was 32 years old that the path became clear, and my passion and profession melded into one. I had been fired from my job and an hour later I had a heart-to-heart conversation with God. I knew what I had to do, and within eleven days I was driving across the country to start my own business.

One of the most important things I have learned since then is that our identity is not wrapped up in what we do. I am a Christian who coaches baseball, not a baseball coach who is a Christian. Jesus Christ is not only my Lord and Savior, but also the foundation of my life. When things are crumbling around me, He is my bedrock who I go to in times of need.

The title and first five chapters of this book are named after an acronym that I created for a keynote speaking event in 2008. I wanted to give those in attendance something simple to remember and hopefully at the same time make a difference in their lives. I have always loved acronyms growing up and put many of them in my locker or baseball hat to inspire me. When the situation fits, I try to find ways to use acronyms to send clear and straightforward messages to the players I teach and when speaking at an event.

Each chapter in this book is structured where I introduce a point in the beginning and then it continues with the story of how God inspired me to start a business coaching baseball. My heart has always been tied to the game of baseball since I was young, and now I had the opportunity to see if I could do it for a living. God opened the door with the vision He gave me. Now I had to walk it out in faith and get to work building it.

So many individuals have helped shape me into the man I am today. I have grown into the husband, father, coach, and business owner because of them. Some of these people still speak into my life, while others have gone on to a better place. The impact they made is indelible and will forever be a part of me. It is my hope that this book will light a fire inside you and encourage you to not only dream for something more for your life, but to go out and make it happen as well. You can do it!

Take the first step **T O D A Y!**

Take action

Go After What You Want

Overcome

You Will Have Doubters and the
Biggest One Could Be You

Dream

Shoot High and See Yourself
Accomplishing Your Goal

Achieve

Now The Hard Work Starts

Yes

No is Just Another Opportunity for Yes

T

TAKE ACTION

Go After What You Want

This is the first and possibly most difficult step we take when we are making a career decision. I believe that deep down all of us want to work in a field that we are passionate about. We want to love what we do and look forward to going to work each day. Making a difference in the lives of others by practicing our craft brings us joy and is a benefit to our world. Once we identify these passions and make the decision to follow them into a career path, we need to be courageous in our walk and stay focused on what we want to do. We need to move forward and do it.

However, some of us allow fear to enter our minds which keeps us from acting on the passion that is in our heart. Instead of taking a risk and continuing to move forward, we choose the path of least resistance. We decided to stay on the sideline and watch everyone else play in the game. Some of us get paralyzed thinking about the bad things that might happen, instead of focusing on what great things could happen. We fall victim to paralysis by analysis. A huge part of taking action is having faith in your plan.

Faith is defined as having complete trust or confidence in something or someone. You have thought long and hard about this plan and now it is time to step out in faith. Action is required. The dream is in your heart, so now you need to move!

"Now faith is confidence in what we hope for and assurance about what we do not see."
Hebrews 11:1 (NIV)

15

Regret brings more pain to people than failure ever does. I look at what some people call failure and I see it as an opportunity to get better. The key thing is to learn from your mistakes and forge ahead. Jim Rohn said it well in his famous quote, "We all must suffer from one of two pains: the pain of discipline or the pain of regret. The difference is discipline weighs ounces while regret weighs tons."

One of my favorite verses in the Bible is found in the book of Hebrews. In Hebrews 11:1, Paul tells us that "faith is confidence in what we hope for and assurance about what we do not see". When you dissect this verse the two main words that stand out to me are hope and assurance. I believe the main difference is certainty. To me assurance is when I am supremely confident in something and free from doubt. It is an unshakeable belief. I think hope has more of an emotional attachment to it. You must believe in your plan and move forward with action.

For a long time, I kept a small plastic card in my wallet that my sister Mary gave me. I read it nearly every day until the words were rubbed off and barely legible. On it were inspirational quotes that talked about having a sense of urgency in all facets of your life. When you are in an urgent situation, immediate action is required. At some point, we need to apply actions to our passions and move towards our goal. I believe this is of upmost importance when taking on a new profession, whether it is your first or forty sixth job. You need to realize the magnitude of the situation and then act on it.

Aeneas Williams spoke at my church about ten years ago. He is an NFL Hall of Fame cornerback who followed his passion for Jesus and became a pastor. The message he gave us that day made a huge impact on my life. Aeneas told us that when we are pursuing something in life, we need to take the necessary steps towards our goal and then leave the rest to God. It requires action! We gather information, do our best to construct an intelligent game plan, and then move forward. Then, after we have taken these steps and prayed about our situation, we leave the final result to Him. We let go of what we want and let God take care of it. My grandmother taught me to "Let go and let God."

I believe that God can do anything. I have witnessed miracles where people have prayed for something and God delivered, so I would be a liar if I said any different. However, I also know that God is also not a genie in a bottle that we can rub and expect our wishes to come true. He created us in His image to carry out His works on the earth and we need to show our faith in Him through our actions. His timing may not always be how we like it, but who are we to judge God?! He knows what we need when we need it.

Everything in your life will not be planned out perfectly. Life would be so easy if the map was already drawn up and all we had to do is follow the directions to our destination, but how awful and boring would that be! Sometimes situations are thrust upon you, and you have no alternative but to decide which path to take. That is where urgency comes in to play. Some of us must be put into an uncomfortable position to get us to move. That is exactly what happened to me.

THE JOURNEY BEGINS WITH ONE STEP

On March 13th, 2006, I was fired from my job at Musashi Auto Parts in Battle Creek, Michigan. It is a large factory that manufactures automatic transmission gears for Honda. My title was Project Coordinator and even though I tried very hard to fulfill my responsibilities to the best of my ability, things did not work out and I was let go. I was now in a position where I could not afford my bills. I didn't like my past two jobs and I disliked the town I lived in. Life seemed hopeless. So, what did I do? I prayed.

Seven months prior to getting fired from Musashi, I got serious about my relationship with God. On August 21, 2005, I was baptized by Pastor Lee Cummings in Lake Campbell at our church picnic in Kalamazoo, Michigan. The next day was my birthday and after work I went to go hear John Wooden speak at the University of Western Michigan. Coach Wooden is in my opinion the greatest

17

coach of any sport all-time. During his coaching tenure at UCLA, the basketball team won 10 National Championships. His .804 winning percentage overall as a head coach is mind boggling.

Coach Wooden's speech was amazing, and it started to stir something inside me. I spent the next half hour driving home realizing how much I hated my job. I felt out of place there and didn't like putting on a fake smile every day. I wanted to do something else with my life and I missed being involved with baseball. On August 23rd I got fired from my job at Enterprise-Rent-A-Car. Funny how sometimes you get what you wish for, but the timing is not quite what you expected.

Soon after getting fired one of my friends from church came over to my home and started asking me some tough questions. What do you want to do with your life? What are you passionate about? How can you go about accomplishing these things? From that conversation I realized that I wanted to start a baseball academy, but I had some roadblocks. The biggest one was I didn't think the area I lived in would be a good fit because of the lack of clients. Therefore, I would need to move.

The problem with moving was the fact that I was living in a house that I couldn't sell for six more months unless I wanted to pay capital gains taxes on the profit I made selling it. I had put a lot of work into the house and didn't want to lose that money. Even though I wanted so badly to get back into baseball I decided the time wasn't right and I needed to start looking for another job in Battle Creek. I continued to pray after my friend left and during this time the Lord stepped in and gave me a word. He just said "Cactus". I heard it in my head, and I wasn't sure what it meant, but I filed it away in my memory.

I went through a month of not working and diligently went to the unemployment office daily. It was a very discouraging time in my life and a lot of anxiety started to build up inside me. No jobs seemed to be a match and I was losing hope. Then around the beginning of the fourth week two of my buddies that I worked out with at the gym got me an interview at Musashi. I met with the hiring board only once and from that interaction I felt secure that the job was mine.

Earlier in the month one of my best friends from high school, Troy Theall, had sent me a free plane ticket to come back to Phoenix, so I decided to fly home. The day after I landed Musashi called and offered me the job. I let them know I could start in a week and had one of the best vacations of my life. Not only was I getting at 20% increase in pay from my last job, but I also worked 10 less hours per week. God is so good!

On most days I didn't enjoy my new job, but it was paying the bills and I had started to build a vision for the future. One of the perks of the job was a membership to the local YMCA and they had an indoor batting cage right off the basketball courts. In January of 2006, I started to throw into the net and hit off the tee a few times a week. I was involved with a charity that raises money for Little League baseball in Arizona and every year we have an event in early February that includes a dinner, an auction, a golf tournament and baseball game. I worked out only because I didn't want to look foolish at the game.

A funny thing started happening when I would enter the cage. Random kids would just open the net without permission and ask me to throw them a ball. I was a complete stranger, but they didn't care. It shocked me at their bravado, but I was like "sure", so I pulled out my extra mitt and started to play catch with them. I would give them pointers and after a little while they would decide to leave and go shoot some hoops on the court. I didn't know it then, but God was giving me a little insight on what was to come.

The trip to Arizona in February was great and I made the decision that I would move back to Phoenix and start teaching baseball again once my house sold in Michigan. It was now at the two-year mark from the time I bought the house, so I put it on the market and waited for it to sell. I figured within six months my house would be sold and I would be back home in the desert. The funny thing is God decided that I needed to get back sooner and that takes us full circle to March 13th.

I was taken into a small room with two other people on this Monday morning, and was told to leave effective immediately. They escorted me back to my desk and I took my belongings in a small box and drove home with a sick feeling in my stomach. I started asking God "Why is this happening now? The house hasn't sold yet. Why are you letting this happen? I thought we had a deal. Once the house sells, I'm outta here to start teaching baseball like you told me to do!"

What I needed was a moment to collect my thoughts and relax. I realized that I was talking to God like he's my buddy and not the creator of the universe. This is blurring the lines like when a child disrespectfully barks back at their father. The last time I got fired I freaked out in the third week and was feeling desperate and all alone. This time I decided to get quiet and pray to God in the manner that He deserves. Then something amazing happened as I stood in my kitchen. I started to have a conversation with God.

The room was silent, and I felt very calm. God asked, "What month is it?" I answered March. Then He asked, "When does Little League baseball start in Arizona?" I answered March again. His next words were so simple yet nearly brought me to my knees. He said "GO!" I immediately felt peace. I believed that God wanted me to start a youth baseball business in Phoenix, so I started getting to work on His plan immediately.

The next eleven days were a complete blur. The first thing I did was call my old boss, Jeff Rodin, at the Arizona Diamondbacks. I told him I was moving back to Phoenix, and I inquired about my old position as an independent contractor for their baseball camps. I had worked for the D-Backs from 2001 through the spring of 2003 and enjoyed my time with the organization. He welcomed me back and asked me how fast I could get home. As a matter of fact, I ended up meeting Jeff in Los Alamos, New Mexico on my upcoming ride back to Phoenix and helped him run a coaching clinic there.

Now that I had some work lined up, I needed a different vehicle. My 1993 Thunderbird was not going to make the 2,000-mile trek across the country. It had over 190,000 miles on it, no taillights, the heater stunk, and to top off it was rear wheel drive. In slick or icy conditions, it was like driving a toboggan backwards. In the winter I kept sandbags in the trunk to keep the car from sliding off the roads. Remember it was March in Michigan so having a snowstorm was always a possibility that time of year.

I remembered a message that Pastor Lee had given that encouraged us to pray specifically for our needs and the Lord would meet them. I had never done this before, but I felt that this was the right time. I prayed for an SUV that was in good condition, had 4-wheel drive, cost less than $7000, and I wanted it to be white.

I figured if the vehicle is white, the company logo I would eventually put on it would stand out better. I had an equity line on my house that only had $7000 left on it, so I couldn't afford any more. Two days later I found an ad in the local paper that blew my mind.

"This is the confidence we have in approaching God: that if we ask anything according to his will, he hears us."
1 John 5:14

The ad said something to the effect of 2002 Ford Explorer for $8000 or $6000 plus your car. It was a 4-wheel drive, in mint condition and you guessed it, white as new fallen snow. The guy selling it came by my house and we drove the vehicle over to my mechanic. The mechanic said if I didn't buy it, he would; so, the negotiations started. We ended up agreeing on $6600 and my living room furniture. I was trying to sell it anyway and the amazing thing was that my furniture matched the guy's freshly painted walls and new carpet in his home! The next day I went to the Department of

21

Motor Vehicles and the title and license fee was exactly $400. My mind was totally blown.

I tried to rent a U-Haul later in the day, but they said they don't rent to people with Explorers anymore because of roll over issues. I took a deep breath and instead of worrying I called up my good friend Bill Crawford and on Saturday we went to Menards to buy a trailer and some wood. The trailer was very shallow and had no real walls to it. I needed to haul a bunch of storage bins back home, so we had to modify it. Bill could fix or build pretty much anything, so we sat out in front of his house and built four-foot walls out of plywood and secured them with 4 x 8 planks. Boom! New trailer.

On Sunday I went to Resurrection Life Church for the last time. I was so excited to tell Pastor Lee and all my friends what was happening, but I had to wait until after the service. Aside from the pastor's great speaking ability, the thing I loved about the church was the worship team. At the end of the last song, they sang the chorus "Christ within us" over and over again. As I sang something amazing happened and I heard the Lord once again say "Cactus". I was shocked because this time He revealed the meaning to me. The word is an acronym, and it stands for **C**hristian **A**thletic **C**amps Chris**t** within **US**. The letter "t" in the middle of the word doubles as a cross and therefore is in lower case.

I wrote the word down in my notebook along with its meaning. After the service I showed what I had written to Pastor Lee's executive assistant. His assistant just happened to be the wife of my friend that I prayed with in my house seven months earlier. I believe God sent him specifically to stoke a fire and passion for baseball in my soul again. She asked if the church could keep the piece of paper and without hesitation, I tore it out of my notebook for her. Pastor Lee was thrilled at the news and told me that I was starting a ministry out of the church. I just saw it as a job, but he knew it was more than that.

By Thursday I had either sold or given away all my possessions except for some clothes and personal belongings. I packed my two dogs (Bocephus & Harley) and two cats (Indy & BC) into the Explorer and by midafternoon I was driving through a small snow flurry on my way home to Arizona. I was immediately thankful that the Thunderbird was no longer in my possession and could hardly wait to leave my old life in the rearview mirror. The house had not sold yet, but my mom would welcome me at her place with open arms until I was able to afford my own home in Phoenix. God was moving me at warp speed, and I liked it!

Explorer with Our Cactus Logo

In my situation I was forced into action. I had no alternative because the words failure, mope and pity are not associated with my vocabulary anymore. I prayed about the situation, searched for wisdom, and then took action steps towards my goal. God gave me marching orders to leave Battle Creek and the vision to start Cactus. I did this out of obedience because He is my ultimate leader. No matter what you are facing, it's not too big or too powerful for God. Stay focused on Him and the plans He has for your life.

"I can do all things through Christ who strengthens me."
Philippians 4:13 (NKJV)

LIFE APPLICATION

1. Have faith in your plan.
2. Walk out your faith with action.
3. Have a sense of urgency.
4. Surround yourself with people who hold you accountable.
5. Spend quiet time with God on a daily basis.

NOTES:

_____

_____

_____

_____

_____

_____

_____

_____

_____

_____

_____

_____

STUDY QUESTIONS

1. What do I really want to do for a career?
2. How can I make money doing it?
3. How will this career bless others?

NOTES:

O

OVERCOME

You Will Have Doubters and the
Biggest One Could Be You

Self-doubt is one of the biggest killers of dreams known to man. It has shipwrecked voyages before they ever left the port and turned carefully thought-out plans into heart wrenching regrets. It is bad enough when you have people telling you that you can't accomplish something, especially when they are family and friends. The real punch to your gut is when you start to doubt your own talents and believe them.

Over the years I have coached baseball players of all ages. When I started Cactus back in 2006, most of the athletes I worked with were under the age of twelve. This brought me into the world of childish hijinks, and I was quickly reminded of how honest and brutal kids can be when they talk to one another. The childhood phrase, "Sticks and stones may break my bones, but words will never hurt me" turned into one of the topics I would discuss with our players during our "team talks" at the end of a clinic. Words do hurt and can leave a lasting impression on people for a long time. Developing a negative mindset is something we must learn to overcome.

One thing you need to realize is that most of the people who doubt you suffer from a lack of vision, a fear of the unknown, or jealousy of your talents. In certain situations, it may be a combination of all three. They are afraid to take risks and get out of their comfort zone. Some people would prefer to stay in an uncomfortable situation and complain about it instead of making

27

a positive move forward into unknown territory. It takes a lot of guts to take risks, and not everyone is willing to make the sacrifices necessary to accomplish what they need to do to reach their goal. When someone does, I call it "stepping out of the boat".

In the Bible there are many stories about taking risks and stepping into uncharted territory. One of my favorites is in Matthew Chapter 14:22-33. This tells the story of when Jesus feeds the five thousand. Jesus sends his disciples out on a boat while He dismisses the crowd and then goes on to pray by Himself. When Jesus is done, He notices the boat is far away from where He is at, so He walks out to it on the sea. When they first see Jesus, their initial reaction is fear because they don't recognize Him. They think He is a ghost. Jesus tells them to "Take courage! It is I. Do not be afraid."

Peter recognizes the voice of his teacher and says, "Lord if it is You, command me to come to you on the water." The response from Jesus is simple and direct, "Come." That one-word command reminds me of when God told me to "GO!" and it brings a smile to my face even to this day. Science tells us that what is about to transpire is impossible, yet Peter's faith in Jesus allowed him to take steps on top of the waves that were crashing into the boat he was in. Imagine how much courage and faith that took!

Now as you read on, the story tells us how Peter saw the wind was violent and he became scared. He then started to sink, and Jesus reached out his hand and caught him. Self-doubt and his surroundings kept Peter from continuing to walk out and meet Jesus. These types of distractions are similar to the things that keep us from accomplishing our goals. This story also reveals to us that as we show faith in God to take a risk, He is always there to catch us when we fall. He never judges us, no matter what we do. What He wants us to do is take that first step towards Him. God wants us to have faith in Him.

"Immediately Jesus made the disciples get into the boat and go on ahead of Him to the other side, while He dismissed the crowds. After He had sent them away, He went up on the mountain by Himself to pray. When evening came, He was there alone, but the boat was already far from the land, buffeted by the waves because the wind was against it.

During the fourth watch of the night, Jesus went out to them, walking on the sea. When the disciples saw him walking on the sea, they were terrified. "It is a ghost!" they said, and cried out in fear. But Jesus spoke up at once: "Take courage! It is I. Do not be afraid." "Lord if it is You" Peter replied, "command me to come to you on the water." "Come," Jesus said.

Then Peter got down out of the boat, walked on the water, and came toward Jesus. But when he saw the strength of the wind, he was afraid, and beginning to sink, cried out, "Lord, save me!" Immediately Jesus reached out His hand and took hold of Peter. "You of little faith," He said, "why did you doubt?" And when they had climbed back into the boat, the wind died down. Then those who were in the boat worshiped Him, saying, "Truly You are the Son of God!"

Matthew 14:22-33 (BSB)

Overcoming doubt and stepping into the unknown, can be the most frightening part of any journey. However, I believe that it takes great risks to receive great rewards. A friend once told me that nothing worth having in life is ever easy. As I reflect on my life, I can see that most of the things that I accomplished took not only risk, but also very hard work. If you are willing to put in the work, you will see positive results.

So, before we get back to the origin story of Cactus, I want to turn back the clock to a time in 1998 when my work ethic and love for playing the game of baseball professionally was put to the test. It was a complete physical and mental gut check and there were days when I thought my playing career was over.

1998

In February of 1998, I tore the labrum in my right shoulder. I decided to play in a semi-pro football league that winter and during the first game of the season I was blindsided on a punt return. I immediately knew something was wrong, but I finished the game and played the entire season with the injury. This was my throwing arm, and my range of motion was limited to less than twenty five percent of what was considered normal. I knew in my heart that the ability to play in the minor leagues that year was in jeopardy.

I began to rehab the shoulder immediately and worked out for at least two to three hours per day. Within three months I was able to throw out to around 120 feet, which is nearly the distance from home plate to second base, but my arm strength was clearly not what it used to be. I reported to an independent minor league team for their spring training in North Dakota at the end of May. I was released within two weeks. I was offered a plane trip home but declined to go. I flew to Minneapolis, MN and from there, I took a bus to my cousin's house in Kalamazoo, MI and worked out for a team there. They said no. I headed down to another team in Chillicothe, OH and received the same news after practicing with them for nearly two weeks.

I eventually signed with a team in Tupelo, MS. I was playing well, but the team ownership was in disarray and the franchise folded while we were on the road. I moved in with a teammate in Canton, OH and we were both determined to find somewhere to play. I signed a "weekend contract" with a team in Huntingburg, IN, but was asked to leave after the three games. Still determined to play I agreed to sign with a team in Bend, OR and paid for the plane flight myself. When I arrived, I practiced with the team, but the contract that was promised never came to fruition. I talked the manager into allowing me to stay in Bend and work out for other teams. I literally lived at the ballpark.

During my time there, I slept either in the clubhouse or on a couch on top of the first base dugout. Yes, you heard me correctly, ON TOP OF THE DUGOUT! My diet consisted of cereal, peanut butter, hot dog buns, and leftovers from the concession stand. For about ten days, I worked out for opposing teams and eventually was asked to leave when no one offered me a contract. I took a 29-hour bus ride back to Phoenix with a bruised ego, but a desire to still play. When I arrived home two days later, I continued to stay in shape and contact teams. A manager from Johnstown, PA agreed to give me a look and said to meet the team for their three-game set in Canton, OH. With the promise of only a tryout, I drove my car all the way to Canton.

The trip took 3 days and I stayed with family in Oklahoma and Kentucky along the way. One of my best friends, Troy Theall, came along for the ride for some moral support. He was a teacher, so he had the summer off and believed that I could do this. Troy stepped in when I really needed him, and it made the trip so much better. After staying the second night in Louisville with my sister Mary, I dropped Troy off in Indianapolis so he could fly back to Phoenix. As he got out of the car, Troy gave me an envelope full of $20 bills. He said it was from his dad with the message to keep fighting.

When I finally arrived in Canton, I slept in my car to save money. I originally considered parking my car at a city park, but after some thought I pulled into a hotel and stayed the night in the parking lot. I wanted to save the cash that Troy's dad gave me. I worked out with a few other players for the Johnstown team on Saturday and the Canton team on Sunday. Neither team made me an offer. I thought maybe it was time to call it quits for the summer, until God stepped in.

A player who did get an offer that weekend from one of the teams came up to me and asked me how I was doing. I was very transparent with him and told him about my year. He invited me to dinner with a group of his friends and since I had nothing better to do, I accepted. When we were about to leave the restaurant, the

31

real shocker came. He invited me to come live with him. Who does that?! We had never met before that weekend, but he believed in me and said that I would end up signing with someone. It was the lifeline I needed at just the right time.

I moved into his house in Cleveland and slept on his couch. He offered me food, shelter, and a place to work out. I read inspirational Christian books and played darts against myself in the basement. About ten days later I received a contract offer and agreed to play for the New Jersey Jackals, an Independent League team in Montclair, NJ. On my way there I made a phone call to one of my college teammates because I knew he was from Jersey. As it turned out, he lived only fifteen minutes away from the baseball stadium and he invited me to stay at his house. God showed up again.

It was now August, but there was still a month left in the season. The team kept me as a utility player because I could catch, play the infield, and the outfield. I didn't play that much, but I was happy to be wearing a uniform and I bonded quickly with my teammates. The manager loved my fighting spirit, and it gave me a lot of confidence. We ended up going to the playoffs and won the Northeast League Championship! It was an amazing way to end a very challenging summer. God is so good!

I decided to stay in New Jersey that offseason and got into prime physical shape. My shoulder was healed, and I was in a great place both mentally and physically. The following March I showed up to a tryout in Tucson, AZ with the Chicago White Sox. There were about thirty-five players in attendance. I was the only one to sign a minor league contract with them that day. They literally sent me to the clubhouse after the tryout, put a uniform on me, and I joined the other players for the start of spring training. Eight months earlier I was sleeping on a dugout. Now I was with a Major League team!

One thing to remember when you are going through a storm in life is to be patient with the timing of when you will see the results come to fruition. Today's unfinished project will be tomorrow's priority. It can't be completed yesterday, and it probably won't be perfect tomorrow. Remember to enjoy the ride and not focus only on the destination. You just might miss all the beautiful scenery along the way.

When it came to starting my business, I took the first step by listening to God and moving to Phoenix. I was so excited about what the future had in store for me that I didn't think about the roadblocks I was going to have to overcome early on.

IT'S BETTER TO WALK BEFORE YOU SPRINT

The move from Battle Creek to Phoenix took three days. Once I arrived home, I started coaching spring break baseball camps for the Diamondbacks and had a steady income for the next four weeks. I expressed to my boss Jeff that God had given me a vision for a business and that I was going to go off on my own sometime this year. He encouraged me to do so and let me know that I was always welcome to work for him, which I did over the summer.

There was a two-month gap between the spring break and summer camps, which meant there was no income until June, so I needed to plan for that. I had done a lot of baseball lessons when I worked for the Diamondbacks from 2001-2003, so starting those back up was the most obvious choice. I called my old clients to let them know I was back in town and available to do individual and group baseball training again. None of them took me up on the offer. Some didn't even return my phone message. I was starting from scratch, and it was going to be a tough road. Thank God Momma Horton was giving me free food and shelter.

Jeff always encouraged the coaches to promote themselves at each of the camps and at the end of the week and allowed us to pass out our business cards for lessons. A few of the parents showed some interest and within a couple of weeks I started training some younger players at a batting cage in my friend's back yard. I would attend their baseball games to check on their progress and through this met other parents who wanted their sons to work with me. Now I had a small base of clients and just enough money to make ends meet.

Every business, especially one that is sports related, has a logo. At this early stage I did not have one on paper, only in my mind. When I started out, I was determined to change the lives of everyone I met through Christ using baseball as the vehicle. I was going to promote the Christian aspect of the business and hoped to attract the large amount of people who attended church on a regular basis. The logo I had envisioned was a cross with a sunburst behind it. I also wanted to incorporate a fish in it as well, which is well known as a symbol that identifies with Christianity.

The people helping me design the logo tried to encourage a different route, but I knew what I wanted. They sent me a bunch of ideas and we agreed on a design relatively quickly. I qualified for a small business loan and started thinking about the next step. I dropped a bunch of money on shirts, hats, and a website. I hadn't even done an event yet, but I was going to be ready when we started. I didn't realize it, but I was starting to allow my emotions and the excitement of starting a business take center stage. I lacked wisdom and taking counsel from others.

Original Cactus Logo

My house in Michigan sold in June and the money I made on it paid off most of my personal debt. The location I did lessons at and the church I attended was in Scottsdale, which is thirty miles away from my mom's house. I was logging close to four hundred miles per week in my Explorer, so it made sense to buy a house there. I closed on a home a month later and there was a school only a block away. The school's baseball fields were used by a local Little League and guess what the name of it was- Cactus Little League.

The league was hosting an All-Star tournament, so for about a week I would walk over and introduce myself to people. I found out that they played in District 3 and contacted the president. We hit if off right away and talked about what I was trying to do. He told me that all the league presidents within the district would meet once a month and invited me to come speak at their next meeting. This was huge for me in so many ways.

A couple of weeks later I was standing in front of ten league presidents from District 3. If the average league has three hundred players in it, I now had the ability to reach three thousand players! I had all my business cards and flyers ready to pass out and was confident I nailed my presentation. Most everyone took my information and the president from Horizon Little League asked me to call her about doing a possible clinic the following spring. I was pumped!

I spoke with the district president afterwards and he said he liked me a lot. However, he didn't think that he would be able to promote a business that was so up front about its religious beliefs. He had been in Little League for a long time and believed I would be a tough sell. I felt sick to my stomach. I jumped in my truck to drive home and accidentally left my flyers on the top of it. Within half a block of the parking lot they were strewn all over North Phoenix. I felt like Charlie Brown when Lucy pulls the football away when he is trying to kick a field goal. AAUUGH!!!

What was I going to do? I spent a lot of time and money already and to top it off my website designer was extremely busy. It took him more than two weeks to do simple updates and I was reeling at this point. So, instead of freaking out I went to the bible and searched for answers. In Proverbs 15:22, it talks about searching for wise counsel, so I decided to talk to my pastor, Troy Johnson, and asked him what he thought.

> **"Plans fail for lack of counsel, but with many advisers they succeed."**
> **Proverbs 15:22 (NIV)**

We sat down in his office, and he started asking me questions. We talked about the past couple of months and the logo design. He then got down to the point. "What word did God give you, Billy?" I replied "Cactus". He asked if God gave me a vision of the logo and I said no. It was just my idea. He then opened the bible to Matthew 10:16. The verse says to be "wise as serpents and harmless as doves". In this context the serpent is viewed in a positive light as crafty or shrewd. Someone who is creative and relatable. The dove represents us not judging others and reaching people where they are in their life.

Pastor Troy reminded me of why I took the risk of starting the business in the first place. He got me back to square one and the focus shifted to using baseball as the vehicle to reach people and away from what the logo looked like. If I wanted to share Jesus with people, they should know He lives inside me by the way I act and speak. I don't need a cross on my hat to let them know that. A friend once told me, "If you were put on trial as a Christian, would there be enough evidence prove you guilty." Let that simmer in your dome for a while.

One great thing that did come out of that first round of t-shirts was an inspirational phrase we put on the back of them. *"David only needed a sling and a couple of stones. What are you going to use?"* It came to me one day while I was working out and was inspired by the story of David and Goliath in 1 Samuel 17. We still use this quote on our social media today and people love it. My hope is that it will help you as well when you are facing what seems to be an immovable force in your life.

David was a shepherd boy who overpowered a champion warrior and then became one of the greatest kings ever. When he faced Goliath others that were there with him on the battlefield felt that Goliath was too big to hit. David probably felt like he was too big to miss! God can use whomever he chooses to do His work and bless whomever He wants no matter who you are. If God can use someone like me who struggled with self-doubt for a long time, He can definitely use you!

The meeting with Pastor Troy gave me some great perspective. There is an old saying that says "sometimes you need to take a step backwards to take two steps forward", and that was the direction I needed to go. Even though I had already invested a lot of time and some money into this logo, it needed a different look so I could reach more people. It was time for the company logo to get a facelift and I was looking forward to the direction of Cactus in 2007.

The question I pose to you is "Who's your Goliath?" This may not be a person, but a place or situation. What is holding you back and how are you going to overcome it? The answer is inside you and now it's time for you to get quiet and pray for the Lord to help you unearth it. Remember He didn't reveal what Cactus meant to me right away. It took seven months! God works in His own time, so be patient and never question if He is there for you. He always is and typically is the one carrying the bulk of the weight. If you have not read the poem "Footprints" I encourage you to do it. It is a beautiful depiction of God being there for us when times are difficult.

"This is my command—be strong and courageous! Do not be afraid or discouraged. For the LORD your God is with you wherever you go."
Joshua 1:9 (NLT)

LIFE APPLICATION

1. Search for the positive in every situation.
2. Be careful with the words you say and the tone you use.
3. Seek wisdom and counsel from people you trust.
4. Narrow your focus and take one step at a time.
5. Be patient and trust God's timing.

NOTES:

STUDY QUESTIONS

1. What risks do I need to take to make this new venture possible?
2. Who do I trust and can go to for wise counsel?
3. Who or what is standing in the way of achieving my goal?

NOTES:

D

DREAM

Shoot High and See Yourself
Accomplishing Your Goal

Dreams are powerful. They give us hope and a vision of where we want to be one day. As children we all had dreams of who we wanted to be one day. Some of you wanted to be a doctor so you could help people and one day cure cancer. Others wanted to play in the NFL, just like the guys who they had posters of on their walls. Maybe you wanted to discover new places and travel the world looking for treasure. Regardless of what your dream was we all shared one thing as kids- fabulous imaginations and the ability to dream big.

Momma Horton used to always tell me, "Shoot for the moon Billy, because if you miss, you'll still end up with the stars." I loved that as a child, and I still use that phrase myself. My mom was very positive and encouraged me in almost everything I did. It was important for me to have someone in my life like that because I was not a very confident person. She could have easily told me how the odds were stacked against a skinny little kid like me and completely crushed the dreams I had for my future self.

I am the father of two teenage boys, and I love their imaginations. Over the years we have talked about what they want to be when they grow up and I smile at the detail of their responses, especially when they were younger. Bryce wanted to be a Major League Baseball player and an archeologist. He planned on digging up dinosaur bones in the off-season. Connor has always loved sports but was also captivated by jets and helicopters. He said he might want to become a pilot. When they asked me if they can do it one day, I always answered "yes". Shoot for the moon boys.

Growing up I was always enamored by professional sports. I remember watching Billy Sims of the Detroit Lions and wondered what it would be like to play in the NFL. My favorite sport was baseball, and the 1984 Detroit Tigers completely captivated me. I would play whiffle ball in our front yard with my friend and switch hit their lineup every game. Guys like Alan Trammel, Lou Whitaker, Chet Lemon, Kirk Gibson, and Lance Parrish. They were who I wanted to be and when I was ten years old, I decided that I was going to be a pro baseball player.

Back then it was just a dream. The plan was to play until I was forty and then retire. I was going to live way out in the country and buy a huge piece of property that my entire family could build houses on. I even planned on naming the street Horton Boulevard. I would retire in peace, and no one would bother me. We would have barbeques every weekend and live the good life. Well, now that I think about it, having my parents, five sisters and two brothers all living on the same street as me would probably not be that peaceful.

The thought of coaching never entered my mind. I loved playing the game. There was something magical and beautiful about the sport. The sound of a wooden bat smacking a ball, the pop of the mitt on a good heater, or reading the hop on a ground ball. It brought me joy and never felt laborious. I had a tremendous work ethic and a high pain tolerance, so I was built for the game. The only record I had my sights set to break was Lou Gehrig's consecutive games played. I loved being on the field and didn't ever want to come off.

The dream of playing professionally came to fruition, but not the way I expected it. Playing twenty years in the big leagues and retiring out in the country at forty did not happen. I ended up going undrafted out of college and eventually signed a free agent contract. I carved out four unremarkable seasons in the minor leagues and at the age of twenty-six, I made the decision to a move on to a new chapter of my life. It was the most difficult thing I had ever done up to that point. The problem was I didn't really have a plan on what the next step was.

Remember, I didn't really want to be coach. If I did, I would have been an education major in college and coached in high school. I loved playing the game and coaching it seemed boring. However, I had some experience over the years working at baseball camps, and for a couple of seasons I helped coach at my high school alma mater. I also recalled how unhappy I was in some of my past management and sales jobs that I worked at in the offseason. So, I decided to give coaching a chance.

I am here to tell you today that it is not only children who have dreams. As adults we dream about what we want to become regardless of what we have been doing up to this point in our lives. Your dream is not dead. It may be covered in years of fear of the unknown or settling for the safe route. However, it is still there. Now what about this. Has your life taken a new direction? Has your dream changed? If so, what has your dream morphed into?

My dream of playing pro baseball didn't turn out the way I wanted it to. However, playing the game in the minor leagues was a resume builder of sorts. I learned more about baseball through my experiences on and off the field. I increased in knowledge which prepared me for coaching. God put a new dream in my heart to start Cactus and I felt like I had a new purpose in life. Instead of wanting to just play the game, I wanted to help others by teaching them what I knew about the game I loved. Now my goal is to help them realize their dream of becoming a big leaguer someday.

EXPLOSIVE GROWTH

When I left Pastor Troy's office that day, I knew what I needed to do. I called the person who came up with the original Cactus logo and let her know that I wanted a new design that was a little less religious. I am sure she was on the other side of the phone thinking to herself, "Duh". We talked about the positive feedback I received from the District Little League meeting and how excited I was for the upcoming spring. We got to work on some ideas and with the help of her husband, the new Cactus Logo was born.

New Cactus Logo

As you can see the cross is still prominent, but not as obvious. It was important for me to still have it in the logo. The designers had a cool idea with the "t" in Cactus and the "A" in Athletic Camps. The "t" represents the cross that Christ died on for our sins. The "A" is a combination of two smaller crosses representing the ones that the men who died next to Jesus were hung on. I am big on hidden imagery, so I was very pleased with the end result.

When it comes down to religion, we need to be careful that we don't get too caught up in being legalistic. All the traditions and hand gestures are not as important as the condition of your heart. God calls us into a relationship with Him. He doesn't want to just create us and then never communicate with us again. If you are a parent, can you imagine investing time with your child and then when they leave the house, you never speak to them again? Of course not! Religion is having a set of beliefs which is important. However, having a relationship with God will always trump this.

The spring baseball season was upon us in 2007 and even though our website still stunk; we had a cool logo that I was proud of. The District Little League president helped promote me to his leagues and the business started to grow. I did a free spring promotional clinic at the park near my house and Horizon Little League came through with a paid clinic in March. From there I ran my own Spring Break Camp and started to branch out to other parts of Phoenix.

Another big break came in the form of a media outlet. I got a phone call from a reporter with the Arizona Republic newspaper, and she wanted to do a story on Cactus. I was so pumped! We exchanged some dates, and I prayed it didn't fall on May 12th, which it did. Why was that not the best day of the calendar year? It was my wedding day. That afternoon I was going to be sharing vows with Taleen Noradoukian and after that we would be gone for a week on our honeymoon. School was letting out the Friday before Memorial Day weekend and our Baseball Summer Camps started in early June. That meant it was now or never to do the story.

It wasn't enough to just sit down and have a conversation with the reporter. She wanted to see me in action, so I started calling up my clients and invited them to a free baseball clinic that I was now offering on the morning of May 12th. I convinced Taleen that everything would be fine, and she agreed to the terms. I owed her big time and payment was probably foot massages for a year. Most of my groomsmen were ball players so they suited up with me and we ran a two-hour clinic that morning. The clinic went great and by the time I had to show up at church, I was completely relaxed.

That year I ran twenty-one different clinics that encompassed a fifty-mile radius. A long way from doing lessons in my buddy's back yard only a year earlier. We also made an agreement with an indoor facility in North Phoenix and started to run summer camps there. This allowed us to make another relationship in the baseball world and it increased our network to more youth baseball leagues.

The facility would advertise our camps in house which eventually increased our customer base.

We were even more successful in 2008 and our income nearly doubled. This allowed me to spend more money on advertising and have someone create a better website. Another article was written about Cactus during the spring and this time my mug was front and center on the front page of the Arizona Living section the Arizona Republic newspaper. I was starting to become known in the Phoenix area as not only a good baseball coach, but also a strong man of character.

Not everything was all roses and rainbows in my life. Taleen and I were in big trouble because of the real estate market, and in July 2008 we lost our home to foreclosure. As a matter of fact, we owned four houses at this time and within one year we lost all four of them. We went from owning our own home and renting the other three out, to renting a home from someone else. The real estate bubble that burst caused the economy to go into a recession and we were hurting financially. To top it off she was eight months pregnant with our first baby.

The biggest mistake I made when I moved back to Phoenix was the lure of making a quick buck. I was concerned that I wasn't going to make enough to live on with Cactus, so I got involved with a friend of mine and started buying properties in the hopes of flipping them quickly. I had no knowledge of real estate, so I had him do all the work while I focused on building the baseball business. Little did I know the economy was going to tank. I was deep in debt and my credit score got hammered. Pretty sure that God said Cactus and not "Go make some quick dough flipping houses." This was going to hurt us for a while.

We moved into our new home which was at least half the size of the house we had just lived in. No more pool and no more batting cage in the side yard of my rental property that I still had access to. Just a tree and a strip of grass that took me five minutes to mow. However, we were healthy and now on September 6th

God blessed us with Connor. I would walk the dogs every night and pray over the neighborhood and our situation. I asked God to give me an idea on another way to impact the baseball world. That's when he blessed me with the Arizona Winter Baseball League.

Back when I was playing baseball in high school there was a fall league that played double headers on Sundays. It was run by local college coaches and scouts and that came to mind as I was praying that cool November night. Cactus was now almost two years old, and I had met a lot of professional ballplayers and coaches during this time. I figured I would just get a flier together, send it out to the local youth baseball leagues and offer an inexpensive winter league with professional players as the coaches. The difference is that we would only be playing one game on Saturdays. I had no idea what God had in store for me.

AWBL Logo

Within three weeks we had over two hundred players register! We did not allow club teams in the league, so everyone had to register as an individual. We had three age divisions that encompassed players between the ages of eight and fifteen years of age. In all we had twenty-two teams and each of them had eleven to twelve players on their roster. Every team had a head coach with professional playing, coaching or scouting experience. We had our player evaluations the first weekend in December, and we did our best to split the teams up evenly. It was like a volcano erupting inside of another volcano. Such an amazing God moment in my life.

"Commit your works to the LORD and
your plans will be achieved."
Proverbs 16:3 (BSB)

The opening day for the league happened two weeks after the player evaluations and it was a moment I will cherish forever. It was amazing to see all these kids playing in a league with our AWBL logo across their chest. It wasn't like we donated money to a youth league, and they put our business name on the back of the jerseys. This was our league and every one of these players were wearing our logo! I was blown away by God's mighty work. I walked between the fields and just enjoyed watching the kids play. Eventually I drove to our other location to check on the older teams. It was amazing.

We didn't have any weekday practices for the teams, so our games were two and a half hours long. We used the first forty-five minutes to an hour as a practice and then played the game afterwards. We wanted the league to focus on player development, so we told the umpires that the coaches had the ability to stop the game for teachable moments. Everything seemed to flow very well during the games, which was a testament to the communication skills of the coaches and umpires. They realized that in order for the players to get better, they needed to be on the same page.

Our inaugural season went outstanding, and we received a lot of positive feedback from parents and players. We received more publicity for our business through an online article written about the league and I really felt good about the direction we were headed. Parents were clamoring for me to do a spring league, but I was not going to try and compete with the other local youth baseball leagues. Plus, most of my coaches were professional players, so they were going to be leaving for spring training in February and play in their own seasons.

Coordinating the baseball league was my first big venture into entrusting other coaches with our business. Sure, I had hired men to help run our camps and clinics in the past, but not to this extent.

An average clinic that we put on might have forty kids in it. Now we had around two hundred fifty kids playing in games on the same day, at the same time in different locations, and I was responsible for all of them! Early on I just delegated responsibilities to these men, but then would sometimes get frustrated with the results. My expectations were not met, but it was my fault. I needed to do a better job of developing these coaches and teach them how to run practices the way I wanted them to. Developing always trumps delegating.

One of my personal mentors is Mike Stanley and he encouraged me in the principle of duplication. My heart is to teach people the game of baseball and I can only be in one place at a time. Mike wanted me to harness that love to instruct others and figure out a way that I could mass produce myself. So, in the spring of 2009 I hired a person from our church to video record and create three separate baseball training DVDs. I felt this was my next step in reaching a larger audience.

Cactus Training DVDs

I thought long and hard about the people I would choose to help me instruct in these videos and ended up hiring six professional players who coached at our camps and in our league. It was hard work and at times very frustrating with all the re-takes, but after about one week of filming we were done. The eight of us ended up having a lot of fun with it and even created a blooper reel that we put on each disc, along with my personal testimony. One DVD focused on hitting and base running. Another one was pitching and catching. The third DVD taught infield and outfield play. Now we could teach people from the comforts of their own living room.

The creation of the winter league brought even more success to our business. We conducted thirty camps and clinics in 2009 and added a fall baseball league that ran from September through mid-November. That led us to change the league name by dropping the word, Winter. We were now known as the Arizona Baseball League. We changed out the "W" for a "Z" in the logo and people knew us as the AZBL. As the fall season ended, we took a break over Thanksgiving and then moved right into the winter season.

AZBL Logo

The winter season showed growth as well. In our first year we only played games in North Phoenix. Now we added a South Division and added a league in Mesa. This expanded our reach which allowed us to impact more people. The teams in the North Division had National League mascots and the South Division were American League. Their seasons were played separately, which included playoffs and championship games. We concluded the year with a North vs South All-Star game and one game World Series between the league champions. Everyone loved it.

For the next several years our outreach continued to grow all over the Phoenix area. The baseball clinics and summer camps fed the baseball league, and the baseball league fed the clinics and camps. Some people registered for one of the events, were impressed with our coaching ability, and then registered for the other. It was a beautiful baseball ecosystem that God provided us.

That's when I decided to extend our reach to other parts of the state.

I love the northern part of Arizona, so we started to offer player and coaching clinics in Page, Flagstaff, and Prescott Valley. The kids in these towns did not have as many opportunities as those in Phoenix and the families really appreciated us coming. The town I grew up in was only two thousand people so having a chance to run clinics in cities like these was special to me. It reminded me of a simpler time in my life and I believe these memories helped keep me grounded.

As youth baseball training was growing around the country, more kids were playing year-round. I was getting concerned with overuse injuries and wanted to put the player's health at the forefront, so a few years after we started the AZBL, I made the decision to modify our fall season. We now focused on more speed, agility, and strength training for our athletes during these two and a half months. We would meet twice on weeknights and once on Saturday mornings. The players started a progressive throwing program in October, and we did offensive and defensive drills on Saturdays. We waited until the winter season to play games.

One thing that attracted people to our business was that we blended a lot of positive messages with our baseball training. We placed an emphasis on being a business that cared about the player as a whole. I came up with the tag line "getting stronger inside and out" and had it added to our logo. I noticed that quite a few sports training businesses had the image of a player in their logo, and I wanted to find a way to do something similar.

Jadd Schmeltzer was one of my clients, and in 2011 the Boston Red Sox drafted him. He was the first player that had been drafted since Cactus started and I thought it would be cool to celebrate that. So, we used a photo of Jadd during one of our pitching lessons and had our design expert morph it into the image just to the right of our business name.

GETTING STRONGER INSIDE & OUT

Updated Cactus Logo with Jadd

The focus of our business was to reach as many players as possible and make it affordable to them. We would offer scholarships to players who couldn't afford a camp or the league because it was a "no kid left behind" mentality. Every scholarship would cut into the bottom line, and we did not charge a premium for our services in the first place. While this affected us financially, the smile on a kid's face when they were playing the game they loved was worth it. However, because we didn't charge a lot, I was working my butt off to make as much money as I could and still spend time with my family. I was entering a crossroads with our business, and something had to change.

****

I believe that all of us still have a dream inside. A dream to do great things and help others. The key lies in the end of that last sentence. We are called to be others minded and be a blessing to people. I believe that God has given each of us a dream and it is designed not just for you. He uses our physical bodies on this earth as instruments to do His work. When we are working within the will of God, amazing things happen to us and those that we connect with. Do not let your dream die inside you. Walk out your faith and take the necessary steps towards your goal. God will take care of the rest.

"Let each of you look not only to his own interests,
but also to the interests of others."
Philippians 2:4 (ESV)

52

LIFE APPLICATION

1. Harken back to the dreams of your youth and write them down.
2. Be open to change and be willing to take risks.
3. Stay focused on the impact you will make, not the income.
4. Avoid distractions by keeping your inner circle of advisors small.
5. Be a person who values relationships over being legalistic.

NOTES:

STUDY QUESTIONS

1. What would you undertake if money was not an issue?
2. Has the dream of your youth transformed into something else?
3. Are you supportive of others, or is the focus always on you?

NOTES:

_____

_____

_____

_____

_____

_____

_____

_____

_____

_____

A

ACHIEVE

Now The Hard Work Starts

I have heard that the most dangerous time during a person's journey who climbs Mount Everest is the first day of their descent back down the mountain. I have no data to prove this, but it makes me ask the question; Why? They just conquered one of the most difficult summits known to mankind and probably achieved a lifelong goal. If persevering through hurricane level winds and below freezing temperatures wasn't enough, what in the world besides a blizzard would put them in this much peril? What it might come down to is their mindset.

What typically happens when people accomplish a great feat? Especially one that took a long time, which included a lot of strenuous work. They celebrate! Take for instance winning the World Series. When you include spring training, the regular season and the playoffs, baseball players persevere through over two hundred games in one season. That takes a huge toll on the body mentally, physically, and emotionally. Heck yeah, they celebrate! You see it for yourselves on TV when they are popping champagne bottles and dancing around like little kids. They are living it up.

So, what about the hikers up on Everest. I am sure they are ecstatic once they reach the summit. After soaking in the majestic view and snapping some photos, I assume they will get back to a safe place to celebrate and put in a good night's rest before they make the trek back down. I can only imagine the adrenaline that was pumping through their bodies. However, when they wake up the next day, do they let their guard down a little? This is what makes the decent so dangerous. They get so focused on what it took to get there that they might not keep that same strong mindset on their way down, and then disaster hits.

I believe we are all prone to this. We taste success and then start reading our own press clippings. Maybe entitlement or complacency starts to creep in, and we expect success without continued hard work. We assume that people will continue to be part of the organization we started or a return as a customer. We base our future success on our past accomplishments. That is a dangerous place to be. Have you ever heard the phrase "What have you done for me lately?" I am sure you have. There are two things that are crucial to long term success, and they walk hand in hand together. They are consistency and reliability.

What comes to your mind when you hear the term consistent? Take a minute and ponder this before you read any further. What comes to my mind is the ability to repeat something over and over again with excellence. I have coached baseball for over twenty years from the professional level down to tee-ball. I believe what separates the best players from very good players is their ability to be consistent. At the pro level everyone has talent. Some more than others, but talent alone does not make you a big leaguer. Consistency does.

Players at the major league level have the uncanny ability to perform actions with a high degree of difficulty repeatedly. They learn from their mistakes and are aware of their surroundings, which gives them a mental edge. This allows them to think less and rely on muscle memory. As you can imagine this takes years of practice and a strong mind set. They are always practicing their craft because they know there are well over 150 more minor league players in their organization who are fighting to get to the level they are at.

People want to be part of an organization that has a track record of consistency. Before my wife and I try out a new restaurant, she always goes online and reads the reviews. If the place doesn't have at least four out of five stars, we are probably not going. Do you think someone will respect you as a leader if you are consistently late or using bad judgment? Would you want to work for someone like that? Of course not. Being consistent makes people feel more comfortable.

Let's now talk about reliability. One of my friends who has coached for a very long time has always told me that if you give him a team of reliable players, they will be successful. Guys you can count on and trust. They make the routine plays on defense and take good at bats at home plate. They make good decisions, and you don't have to worry about them going out on the town and making fools of themselves and the team. These are guys who allow you to get a good night's rest during a long season.

When I think of a person or organization who is reliable, I know I can depend on them. They are honest and trustworthy. They will come through when I need them most. That not only brings peace of mind, but it encourages me to recommend them to others. Hearing a good review from someone I know carries a lot of weight. To me word of mouth is more powerful than any billboard your put up on the highway or a commercial on TV. As Cactus grew, we did our best to model consistency and reliability, but as I learned those things can be hard to master.

A TIME OF TRANSITION

It was during 2011 when I was starting to get mentally drained. I would attend and run almost every clinic and camp that we offered. On top of that I ran a two hundred player baseball league that had usually twenty teams in it, and we had multiple locations for our playing fields. I oversaw the following for the Arizona Baseball League alone: website updates, weekly email reminders, field reservations, player registrations, player evaluations, ordering uniforms, weekly practice schedules, game schedules, hiring coaches, hiring umpires, setting up fields, coaching multiple teams, roving between locations, and assisting the other coaches.

As much as I wanted to hand off responsibilities to other people, the profit margin did not allow it. I investigated other revenue possibilities such as league sponsors and website advertisements, but the income received was minimal. Overall, we were making decent money, but not enough to put away savings to someday buy a house again. I needed to earn more income and had to figure out a way to do it. I didn't have many ideas to grow the business without driving myself into the ground, so I started to inquire about coaching opportunities at the high school and college level.

During that year I interviewed for head high school coaching jobs at Pinnacle High School and Notre Dame Preparatory Academy. I also interviewed for an assistant coaching position at Grand Canyon University. I felt like I crushed every interview, but all three came up empty. I put in my resume for the head coaching position at Arizona Christian University, but never got an interview. I was discouraged but kept on pushing. In late August I started sending my resume to all thirty Major League teams searching for a minor league coaching position. Over the next three months I received a glimmer of hope from one team, but the communication between us was minimal.

At the end of October, I made a decision that would change my life. I decided to go on a fast for seven days. I would consume no solid food during this time and offer it up as a sacrifice to God. I felt in my heart that I needed to go deeper in my prayer life and walk out my faith. I wanted to show God that I was serious about landing a position with a Major League organization and I would do whatever it takes to provide for my family. It was time for the rubber to meet the road and have my actions match my faith. In James 2:22 it gives an example of how a person's faith and actions worked together, and their faith was made complete by what they did. This scripture empowered me during the fast.

"You see that his faith and his actions were working together, and his faith was made complete by what he did."
James 2:22 (NIV)

Up to this point, fasting was a monthly discipline for me, but I only went did it once per month for one day. The longest I had ever fasted was two days, so I knew this would be a struggle. I needed to rely on God for mental, physical, and spiritual strength to get through the seven days. I remembered a quote from one of my good friends, Scott Adams, who was our associate pastor. He told me that "A fast without prayer is a diet". This always helped me during my fasts, because when the headaches came it would remind me to pray throughout the day and make sure that I was staying hydrated.

During the fast I felt God pressing me to journal each day's events. Right away I knew what He was doing. God was using these seven days to stretch and strengthen my faith. He was refining me in the furnace and on the other side of the fast, I believed my journal would impact the lives of others. I wasn't sure how, but I wanted to be obedient to Him, so I kept explicit details on everything I was feeling those seven days.

The fast ended the first week of November and I didn't hear from any teams the entire month. Finally, on December 8th I got a phone call from the San Francisco Giants during the Baseball Winter Meetings. They told me if this was going to happen it would be quick. Over the next few days, I had two more phone interviews and then threw batting practice to some minor league players at the Giants baseball complex in Scottsdale. Within a week I was offered a job as a hitting coach in the Arizona Rookie League! The biggest blessing out of all of this was I would be home year-round while I was coaching professional baseball.

Months later God told me to submit my journal to a friend who owned a publishing company. The journal became the foundation for my first book, *7 Day Fast*. The subtitle is *Understanding God's Plan Through Faith and Action*, which was inspired by the James 2:22

verse. It was published in October of 2012, and in February 2013 the book was featured at a prominent Christian baseball outreach event called Tales From The Dugout. The organization purchased one thousand copies and gave them out to men when they entered the building. My wife sat up in the rafters of the auditorium and marveled at what God had done. These people were reading our story.

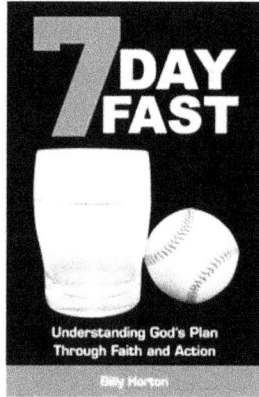

My first book, *7 Day Fast*

My first year with the Giants in 2012 was amazing. Our rookie league team had a very good season and made a run at the playoffs. We came up short, but bigger victories were two months down the road. On October 28th, the Giants defeated my home-town Detroit Tigers in Game Four of the World Series. Words really can't describe what I was feeling. I went from being turned down by local high schools to a member of a World Series Championship organization. The following summer all the minor league coaches were presented with personalized World Series rings made by Tiffany & Co.

Coaching with the Giants allowed me to be home with my family and still run Cactus. The salary they paid me gave us a consistent income and now I was able to hand off coaching and league duties to other men that I had developed over the years. This was a blessing to my family and the men who worked for us.

Now they had more income to provide for their needs. I loved writing checks knowing that the money that was leaving our business account was helping put food on the table for another man's family.

Life was now about learning how to balance things. I needed to figure out how to be a husband and father who is present in his family's life while working full-time for a Major League team, run a business, and do public speaking events. I did my best to master the art of efficiency. I read books and asked other men who were close to me how they did it. My dad was a good man, but he wasn't around very much. By the time I was thirteen, my parents divorced, and I only saw him two weeks out of the year. I was determined to be involved in my boy's lives. Too many of us grew up with an absentee father and we still feel the effects of it today.

During the fall and winter when I wasn't coaching with the Giants, I made sure to take every Sunday off and I didn't check my phone for text messages or emails. If someone called me that day and they weren't a close family member or friend, I didn't answer. I also gave myself set work hours for the business. Once Taleen and the boys left the house for the day I would dig into emails and do my office work. I made sure to be home for dinner at least two or three times per week. I also went to the gym and attended bible studies as often as I could to keep my body, mind, and soul in good condition.

It wasn't always easy, but like I said before, nothing worth having ever is. The coaching job with the Giants helped me in more ways than just the income. I made sure to talk less and listen more my first few years. I wanted to be a diligent listener. The difference between hearing and listening is the comprehension of the information. I learned so much from the coaches around me. The knowledge I gained was funneled back into Cactus which then improved our teaching methods.

When the business first started, I created a coach's manual that I gave to all the people that attended our coaching clinics. Early on

I did these clinics for free and after a couple of years started to charge for them. Inside of it were drills and exercises that I had developed myself and learned from others. Almost every year I would add and remove drills and sometimes modify my teaching methods. I was constantly learning from others, and I wanted to teach people to the best of my ability. I started to refer to the manual as my "noodles" or the results from a boiling pot of spaghetti. I'll explain what I mean by this.

When you are making spaghetti, you need five things: a stove, a pot, noodles, water, and a colander. For starters, we turn the stove on high and put water in the pot. Once the water comes to a boil we toss in the noodles. At a certain point we decide that the noodles are cooked. This is when the colander comes in to play. At this point we dump the contents that are in the pot, the noodles and water, into the colander.

Now let's connect the dots. The conversation you have with someone are the contents inside the pot (water and noodles). The colander is your mind. The things that you agree with are the noodles. What you disagree with is the water. When you disagree with someone it's nothing personal. You simply take the thing or things that you learned and put them in your memory bank to use it later. The other stuff just washes down the drain, maybe never to be seen or thought of again.

The coach's manual became the noodles of everything I learned over the years. I wanted to give other coaches access to the knowledge I learned from people that they may never meet. I knew that through teaching coaches, I would reach more players. The goal is for players to have fun and learn as much about the game as they can. This gives us the ability to empower them with the tools they need to be successful. The game is now about them and not us. We had our time to shine. I get so much enjoyment out of seeing a player smile when they are successful.

Individual success tends to breed team success and in 2013 the Arizona League Giants dominated. We tied a league record for wins, swept the playoffs for the league title and the Giants presented us with championship rings the following spring. In 2014 we had another strong season and went to the playoffs again. This time we came up short losing the championship game to the AZL Indians, but the year would still end with another championship ring. Two days before Halloween the Giants won Game 7 of the World Series in Kansas City, which netted me another World Series ring. I was blown away by the blessings God was providing my family.

2012 World Series Ring
2013 AZL Ring
2014 World Series Ring

More blessings came that winter in a new revenue stream that I didn't expect. A company named ELI Marketing that specializes in large sporting events contacted me through the Cactus website. They needed someone to run an event for the families of ESPN executives during the 2015 Super Bowl that was hosted in Glendale, AZ. On the afternoon of Super Bowl Sunday, we used the Spring Training stadium for the Chicago White Sox and Los Angeles Dodgers to host a fantasy camp. We had a bunch of fun baseball stations for the families to run through and when it ended, they were shuttled to the big game. The event was a huge success, and I was positive that we would work with ELI again down the road.

Things started to change with Cactus later that summer. The client base that attended our summer baseball camps was leaning more towards families in Scottsdale and Northeast Phoenix. For eight years we rented from the same indoor facility for these camps. It was further West than people wanted to travel and that summer we had our lowest attendance since our early years. In 2015 we made the decision to run our camps at another indoor facility that was closer to our client base in North Phoenix and had great success. Our numbers rose significantly that summer and our clients were much happier with the location. I was looking forward to more growth.

The new year brought some new problems. The indoor facility we moved to in 2015 changed ownership towards the end of the year and the new owner told me they wanted to run their own summer camps. This forced us to move again. We found a smaller facility in Scottsdale that had recently opened in the spring of 2016 and made an agreement to do our camps there. They were struggling and welcomed the fact that we brought people into their facility. We enjoyed a strong eight weeks in the summer, but the week after we finished up the facility closed its doors. They went out of business. Where is that football, Lucy and why do you keep pulling it out from under me?! If you love the *Peanuts* comics like I do, you got that reference.

About two miles down the road from me was a multi-sport facility. I made an agreement to do lessons and clinics there over the winter as a trial run. They only had two cages and a soft toss area to do baseball work in. I was used to having eight cages and pitching mounds, so I was not feeling too good about this place. The lessons and clinics went well, and I really liked the general manager and his assistant. They both played baseball and they gave me the ability to do as many lessons as I could handle. It was our new spot for now.

Another unfortunate thing happened and now it was with our baseball league. Our fall training went well, but registrations were at an all-time low for the winter league. We didn't have enough players in any of the age divisions to run the league, so we had to pull the plug after eight wonderful seasons. Club baseball was choking the life out of us with more and more kids playing on their teams year-round. It was getting tougher to rent fields as well and after a lot of thought and prayer the league ended In November 2016.

In 2017, I searched for another facility to do our summer camps, but nothing surfaced. I didn't feel great about the place we were in but agreed to do summer camps there based on the fact I had no where else to go. Our client base did not like the new set up and our camps tanked badly. It was worse than 2014 and the business was struggling. For the first time ever, we didn't offer any camps during the fall or winter, and I was getting very discouraged. I thought about trying to sell the business, but it had lost its value. We were no longer the consistent and reliable business that people had come to know and love.

I felt like a nomad with no place to rest our business' head. If you have been asking yourself, "Why didn't you just open up your own facility?" I understand your thought process. I saw too many of these places go under and it is difficult to make money running an indoor facility. At this point we had finally bought a home for the first time in seven years. The only debt to our name was our mortgage and I did not want to put my family in a position of taking on a large rent payment for an indoor facility. Taleen and I made enough money to provide for our family and for the first time I gave serious consideration to closing the doors on Cactus. Then in the summer of 2018, God intervened.

As you can see the road I traveled with this business has been one with many twists and turns. It reminded me more of the dirt roads I grew up on in West Branch, Michigan than the nicely paved one I drive on now in Scottsdale, AZ. God always had a plan for my life, and I was flexible enough to be open to the changes that came my way. Like a river that has ebbs and flows we need to adjust to the situations we run into daily. Following your dream may not be easy, but the benefits stretch beyond the money you make. The more passionate you are about your craft, the better you will perform it, which blesses everyone you come into contact with.

"In all your ways acknowledge Him,
And He shall direct your paths."
Proverbs 3:6 (NKJV)

LIFE APPLICATION

1. Stay focused and finish what you start.
2. Do your best to model consistency and reliability in everything you do.
3. Prioritize your life with family taking precedence over work.
4. Practice the art of efficiency, which includes making time for yourself.
5. Entrust responsibilities to people by taking the time to develop them.

NOTES:

STUDY QUESTIONS

1. What is your definition of achievement?
2. Are you responsible and can people rely on you? How can you improve?
3. Who can you start to develop so your outreach expands? How will you develop them?

NOTES:

Y

YES

No is Just Another Opportunity for Yes

Do you consider yourself a persistent person? Someone who is willing to fight for what they believe in. The vision is there, and you are willing to do whatever it takes within your power to make it a reality. It takes mental strength to persevere through difficult times. Everything we set our hands to will not be a success but having a long-term focus on the end goal is one of the keys to prosperity. I believe God will close a door to something to protect us and then open another to bless us.

Back in 1995, I received my college degree in Marketing. In one of our classes, we were taught that 10% of the leads we gather will actually turn into sales. That was a bit discouraging for me. At that moment I told myself that I would never take a job that was full commission. It would be too hard and stressful. I wanted to have a guaranteed salary that would bring me some stability and security. Little did I know that about 10 years later I would start a business from scratch.

I think my fear stemmed from hearing the word "no". I was not a big fan of rejection, and I would say that most of us view this word with a negative skew. We started hearing it early on in our lives. As kids we have an inherent curiosity that leads us to figuring out the boundaries of what we can do in life. Some parents joke that they use the word so often, they should just change their child's middle name to no because it follows their first name all day long. "KEVIN, NO!"

Let's flip the script and look at "no" in a positive light. For me it simply means that a yes is around the corner. Hearing no tests our persistence and perseverance. It also allows us to learn about our presentation skills. Sometimes it is not what you say, but how you say it. Tone and body language are two big factors in the way you communicate to others. I see it every day in my own home with the way we speak to our kids and even our hound dog Rusty. He only knows about ten words in the English language, so he normally responds to us by the way we speak to him.

Hearing "no" can be a common occurrence with people who have sales jobs. They are constantly looking for more leads to generate additional possibilities for sales. Not only do they have to find new customers, but also take care of their current clients for repeat business. A "no" to them means they may have to change the way they structure their presentation to that person the next time for a future yes. It is an environment that is populated by hard working grinders who look for innovative ways to gain and retain clients.

Some players and coaches refer to baseball as a "game of failure". I understand what they mean, but the statement drives me nuts. When you look at someone's batting average, anything above .300 is considered good. Therefore, you are failing seventy percent of the time. I prefer to look at it as a game of opportunity. In an MLB regular season, players participate in around 27 games per month for 6 months. That's more than any other professional sport. Therefore, the players receive a lot of opportunities to learn from their mistakes and prove their worth on the field.

When I accepted the San Francisco Giants contract offer in 2011, it wasn't because I was flooded with options. I did not have the luxury of deciding between multiple suitors or who was giving me a better perk package. I received a "no" from twenty-nine other Major League teams and the process took four months. I battled discouragement and anxiety during that season of life but kept my focus on God. He had a plan for my family, and it was going to take time for it to unfold. Ultimately, He placed me in the perfect place at the right time.

We have all overcome difficult situations and persevered through hard moments in our lives. For us to stay determined and focused when we are in the middle of a crisis, we need to stay calm, have perspective, and draw on our past experiences. Learning from these experiences are incredibly important. When you gain victory over a trial, it gives you strength and self-confidence. It is God's way of preparing us for our next battle. I believe there will be seasons of our lives where there is peace and prosperity, but for the most part we are moving from one trial to another.

> *"And not only that, but we also glory in tribulations, knowing that tribulation produces perseverance: and perseverance, character; and character hope."*
> **Romans 5:3,4 (NKJV)**

One thing that I have learned over the years that has helped me immensely is to change my mind set on how I view situations. I do my best to find the positive, regardless of the circumstances. Sometimes you must examine the situation from multiple angles and use creative thinking. It didn't come easy, but sometimes God puts someone in your life to help you gain a tool for your utility belt so you can grow into the person He created you to become.

Jon Huizinga entered my life back in December of 2008. At the time, I was searching for coaches, and he was referred by a friend who owned a baseball complex. I hired Jon to coach one of our baseball teams in the Arizona Winter League that I had just formed. He was a current minor league pitcher and did a great job with the players. They seemed to naturally gravitate towards him and over the next decade we became good friends. However, that first year we coached together, there were times where I just wanted to punch him in the face.

I always took the game of baseball very seriously ever since I was young. It was a passion of mine and I worked very hard at it.

I did not show much patience to those who took the game for granted or showed a lack of effort. When I started coaching, I held the players to a very high standard and when they didn't meet my expectations, I sometimes blew them up. I lacked grace and I didn't always make it fun. With Jon, everything was fun, and he was always so happy. I thought it was fake at first, so it bugged me, but as I spent more time with him, I realized what a genuine person he was.

Jon is the most positive person I have ever met. He is the kind of guy who gets flipped off by someone on the freeway and he waves back with a smile. Nearly every single word out of his mouth is constructive and he always talked about "pumping up someone's tires" by complimenting them. A pitcher could go out and have an awful inning and he would find something positive out of it. His team would make three errors in an inning, and he would be there clapping it up and encouraging them to make the next play. It was so different than what I was used to and so much better than my normal reaction.

He literally changed the way I spoke to players and even my family. Jon made me a better husband and father. He lived out what James taught us in the bible about controlling our tongue. Now I do my best to figure out a way to say things in a positive light all the time. I use it in my everyday life, and it has made me a happier person. I hope that I will be the same person to others, that Jon was to me. The funny thing is this- Jon wasn't trying to affect me. He was just living his life the only way he knew how. As a person who finds the good in everyone and every situation.

"With the tongue we bless our Lord and Father, and with it we curse men, who have been made in God's likeness. Out of the same mouth come blessing and cursing. My brothers this should not be!"
James 3:9,10 (BSB)

My interactions with Jon allowed me to see failure through a new lens. Previously I would look for the bad in a situation so I could find a way to fix it. Now I was looking for the positive so I could build on it to find a solution. We tell our players all the time to continue being great at what they do best and allow us to help them work on their deficiencies. We try and take a weakness that other teams will attack to get them out and do our best to improve that area where one day it can become a strength.

Throughout this book I have mentioned how I heard the phrase "nothing worth having is ever easy". I have quoted that so many times to people over the years. After being around Jon, I decided to change the quote by removing the word nothing and reshaping the phrase using positive words. Now I say, "anything worth having requires hard work". The point is still the same, but now we get rid of the word nothing.

Here are some examples of getting the same point across using positive words.

- *"I look forward to seeing you." instead of "I can't wait to see you."*
- *"Be on time." instead of "Don't be late."*
- *"I'll do my best." instead of "I can't do it."*
- *"Everything is going good." instead of "I can't complain."*
- *"Focus on this." instead of "Don't worry about that."*

STAYING THE COURSE

We started out 2018 well with another big event with ELI Marketing. This is the same company we worked with for the ESPN Super Bowl event a few years earlier. In January I flew to Houston and performed a fantasy camp for the employees of Anadarko Petroleum. This was a celebration of the Houston Astros 2017 World Series win, and in addition to running through our baseball stations, all the employees received a bunch of free Astros gear. Once again, we knocked it out of the park with ELI and I was hoping to partner with them more in the future.

Spring Training was around the corner, and I needed to plan for our summer baseball camps because once March 1st hit, life would get very busy. I needed to have something in place because my coaching job with the Giants was my main work priority. We didn't have a consistent facility for camps anymore and even though the Astros event was a big hit, I had my doubts that the business would survive with another poor showing in the summer. Those camps were the main source of income for Cactus, and we needed them to rebound well.

I was extremely disappointed that our once successful business was now struggling, and the thought of possibly shutting Cactus down was stressful. Then perspective hit me in the center of my chest in May and my positive outlook on life was about to be challenged in a major way. In the middle of the night, I woke up with a sharp pain in my side. Taleen and the boys were fast asleep, so I decided to drive myself to the emergency room. The doctor told me I had pneumonia and that I needed to take a few days and rest so it would not get any worse.

When I got home, I slid back into bed before anyone got up and slept for a few hours. I told Taleen the news and she only believed me when I showed her the hospital wristband. After getting lectured on how dumb I was to not wake her up, I called the Giants to explain what happened and stayed home from work for a couple of days. I wasn't getting a lot better and after a week I had some tests taken and the result was Valley Fever. Essentially it is pneumonia on steroids. My lungs had fluid in them, and my joints were swollen. I was told that it could take up to six to nine months to recover completely.

Now I had to stay home for a few weeks, and I started to get concerned about my job as the manager of the Arizona Rookie ball team with the Giants. They told me not to worry and by the time June rolled around I was back to work in a limited role. I wasn't allowed on the field yet, but I was able to be around the players and coaches in the clubhouse and make the daily schedule. I finally made it back to the dugout on June 24th and in my first game back we beat the Oakland A's at home 4-2. The players doused me with a Gatorade cooler, and I started to slowly get back to a normal routine.

I had some amazing God moments during this time, and He revealed to me things that I needed to work on as a husband and father. I felt distant from God, and I prayed for Him to show me if there was sin in my life that I needed to repent from. He showed me that I was vain and conceited because of my concern that I couldn't workout and I was getting skinny. I became aware that I also lacked empathy for others when they were dealing with sickness or injury especially my wife who was dealing with tremendous back and nerve pain. I got on my face and prayed fervently that He would forgive me.

What happened next within the next two days was a true miracle. The swelling in my joints were gone and my lungs cleared. I went to the doctor at the end of the week, and he said the chest x-ray looked remarkably improved and I would not need the anti-fungal medicine to fight off the Valley Fever. Within ten weeks of the diagnosis my lungs were totally clear, and I was completely healed. No longer did I care if I looked like a bodybuilder. Now I just wanted to live a long and healthy life.

That summer we did not run any camps. I thought about closing the business but something in my heart told me not to. God

75

gave me the vision to start Cactus. Heck, He spoke the word into my heart on two occasions! I decided that I was not going out like a chump and after a lot of prayer, decided to sink some money back into the business and re-vamp everything. Cactus needed a facelift, which included creating a new website.

I also felt led to write more. Over the past decade I shared a story involving a father speaking to his child about how they can honor God with the talents He has given them. My story turned into the poem "Playing for God", and I went through the copyright process during the summer. I needed a home for my written works, so I had a separate website built that was dedicated to me as an author and public speaker. I began to write a men's blog every month and made sure to be very transparent in my writing style. I wanted guys to know that we all struggle, and we are not in this alone.

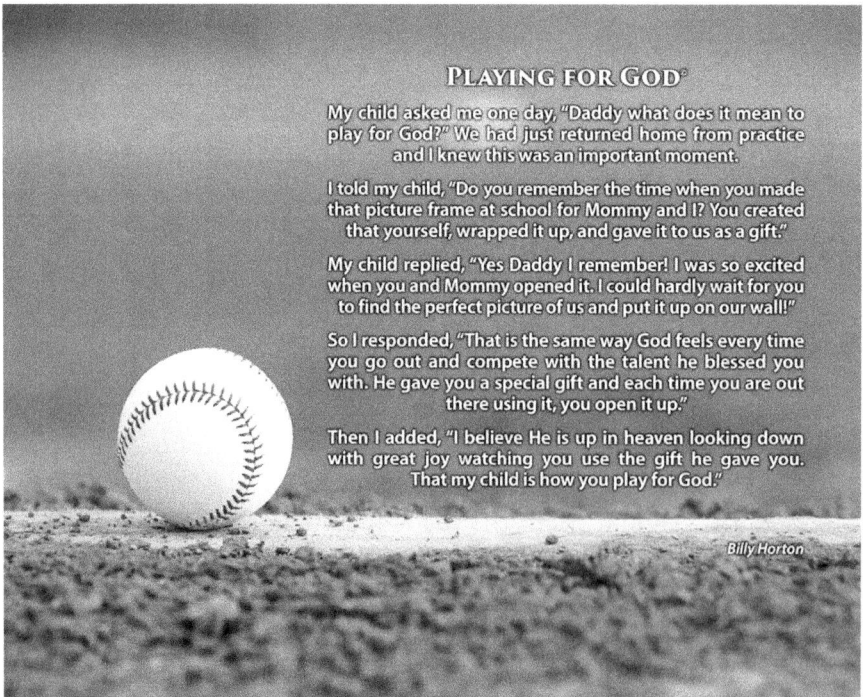

PLAYING FOR GOD

My child asked me one day, "Daddy what does it mean to play for God?" We had just returned home from practice and I knew this was an important moment.

I told my child, "Do you remember the time when you made that picture frame at school for Mommy and I? You created that yourself, wrapped it up, and gave it to us as a gift."

My child replied, "Yes Daddy I remember! I was so excited when you and Mommy opened it. I could hardly wait for you to find the perfect picture of us and put it up on our wall!"

So I responded, "That is the same way God feels every time you go out and compete with the talent he blessed you with. He gave you a special gift and each time you are out there using it, you open it up."

Then I added, "I believe He is up in heaven looking down with great joy watching you use the gift he gave you. That my child is how you play for God."

Billy Horton

The website billyhorton.com was launched in November. I hired someone to teach me about social media platforms and at the same time someone else was helping me build the new Cactus website. We went with a completely new logo, changed our color scheme and I filmed nearly one hundred videos of drills and coaching philosophies. We got a channel on YouTube, and started doing clinics at a new baseball facility that was just down the road from the multi-sport place we were at previously. Things were looking up.

It took a couple of months, but early in 2019 Cactus had a new and improved website. We invested money in advertising by sponsoring local Little Leagues and had a plan for summer camps once again. The indoor facility we were using for our clinics wanted to do their own camps starting in May, but another facility opened two miles away. Undeterred by this new speed bump in our path, we agreed to a contract for the summer with them and experienced success. It wasn't the kind of profit we made in our heyday, but the kids who attended had fun and it was a positive step in the right direction. Cactus was back.

New Cactus Logo

Being determined in life goes well beyond our careers. It is a component of our personal lives as well. Whether it be participating in sports or going after something we want, we all must deal with loss and rejection. How about when you pursue someone you are interested in. Have you ever heard "no" from someone when you asked them out on a date or said you liked them? This has happened to me on a few occasions, but one time in particular it felt like a colossal failure of epic proportions. Here is the story of how my wife and I met, and the epic fail that happened when I asked her out the first time.

TALEEN

When I moved back to Arizona, I was completely happy being single. I focused on starting my business and after a few months bought a house. I had four roommates and really no major concerns outside of building Cactus. Then I met Taleen, and everything changed. I basically saw her everywhere I went. We went to the same church. We attended the same bible studies. I lifted weights five days a week at the rehab center where she worked . She was cute, athletic, and most importantly loved Jesus.

I was convinced that some of our friends were trying to set us up through doubles tennis. We would meet up at least twice per month on a weekend and almost everyone we played against was either dating or married. I thought I was getting signals that she liked me, so I set up a plan to ask her out and tell her about my feelings. I loved having people over and would often have barbeques for family and friends at my house on Aster Drive. Labor Day was approaching so I thought this was the perfect time to approach her. Boy was I wrong.

The following story has been coined "The Labor Day Debacle' or "The Disaster on Aster". You can pick your favorite. There was around thirty to forty people at my house for this barbeque and one of them was Taleen. It was a good mix of my new friends from church and people I grew up with over the years. Prior to everyone showing up, I remember vividly being on my knees in the shower praying to God that approaching her would go well. I really liked her a lot and believed that one day she was going to be my wife.

The party was going well and at a certain point I saw her outside alone. I decided this was the perfect time to go up to her and strike up a conversation. We started out with some small talk and then after a while I told her that I liked her. I said that I had been praying about it and I wanted to get to know her better. At that point, I asked her out on a date. I expected a smile, followed by a slight blush and hearing her say yes. What I got instead was pretty much the exact opposite.

She asked me if anyone else knew about this. Then she followed up by asking me who is holding me accountable in my life. The last thing I remember is her wanting to know if I asked our pastor if it was ok to do this. What?! In my mind I was just asking a girl I liked out on a date and now I am getting grilled by Officer Taleen. We were only a couple of steps from the pool, and I considered pushing her in. I was annoyed, slightly embarrassed, and very uncomfortable. I didn't really answer her questions and after about thirty seconds we had an awkward parting of ways.

Taleen grabbed one of her friends and pulled her into the bathroom to talk. I started washing some of the dishes that were piled in the sink and stared out into the backyard watching my friends have fun. The moment I was in felt like letting the air out of a balloon and hearing that annoying shrieking sound. I went over the sequence of events in my head and laughed at how badly I crashed and burned. The only thing that could have gone worse is if I actually pushed her in.

My roommate asked me what was going on and I just smiled and said nothing. Taleen and her friend exited the restroom and after a rushed goodbye, she left my house. I sat down on the couch to watch some TV, and then the friend she had spoken with came over with her husband. She asked me "What if no, doesn't mean no?" I politely said that I am not into playing games but decided to hear her out. She went on to inform me about how guarded of a person Taleen was. She had a bad experience with her last boyfriend and had not gone out on a date in years.

After our conversation I decided that I should keep pursuing Taleen but take things very slow. Maybe her no, was an opportunity for a yes down the road. It was very awkward the first time I saw her again, and for about a week I kept my distance. Little did I know that during that time she was getting info on me from men that she trusted at the church. Eventually we met for lunch and then played tennis afterwards with some friends. A dinner happened a week later and within two months we began a courtship. This was basically me stating to her that I wanted this to be a serious relationship.

Taleen and I got engaged in December and the following May, she became my wife. We both had some inappropriate relationships in our past and giving in to our flesh was a common mistake we made. Therefore, early on in our relationship we made the decision to save our first kiss for the alter. I felt like if I got to first base in our relationship, that I would keep rounding the bases, and I wanted to treat her like God's daughter. Something I had not done before. The church erupted when I leaned in for that kiss and it was a day I will never forget.

Taleen became the perfect complement to me but in no way does she complete me. Only Jesus does. If Taleen were to die tomorrow, I would be heartbroken, but still be complete because of the decision I made to humble myself and make Jesus Christ my Lord and Savior. That was the most important decision I ever made and if you have not done this, I encourage you to do it today. If you want Jesus to enter your heart it is a simple process. Simply believe in your heart that He is your Lord and Savior and profess it with your mouth.

The decision I made to forge ahead with Cactus was important because I knew God was still using me to do His work in youth baseball. Quitting was not an option. Cactus started to show new growth and we continued to impact the Phoenix community. Writing more on the billyhorton.com website was another new way to impact people. As I was teaching kids how to play baseball, I was also ministering to adults through my online blog. I liked the direction our business was moving and then all the sudden another trial entered my life right before the world was brought to its knees by a pandemic.

****

I recall hearing a sermon where the pastor told the congregation that "No isn't no until God says so!" This phrase encourages us to have faith when times are tough. Those weeks where you feel like you are getting your teeth kicked in repeatedly no matter what you do. The effort is there, but the outcome is not what you expected. You are on your knees praying for an answer, but you haven't seen results yet. Be patient. Know that God is working behind the scenes preparing you for a "YES" that will bless your socks off.

"And all these blessings shall come upon you and overtake you, because you obey the voice of the LORD your God."
Deuteronomy 28:2 (NKJV)

LIFE APPLICATION

1. Stay persistent and fight for what you believe in.
2. Change your speaking patterns to include positive phrases over negative.
3. Be cognizant of your tone and body language.
4. Be innovative and search for a better way to do things.
5. Stay determined and find a way to get it done.

NOTES:

STUDY QUESTIONS

1. What is the first step towards turning your passion into your profession?
2. Who are you going to surround yourself with?
3. Who will you go to when times get tough?

NOTES:

_____

_____

_____

_____

_____

_____

_____

_____

_____

_____

_____

_____

NOTES:

THE SETBACK

Spending Time in the Wilderness

The outdoors is my passion and I love spending time in the wilderness. The quiet of the forest relaxes me and the smell of pine trees invigorates my soul. I enjoy taking long walks with God and having quiet time with Him. I seem to hear his voice so much better out in His creation, and at times I can feel His presence. My family likes to go hiking with me and explore different parts of our beautiful country. Some of the hikes were easy, while others were much more challenging.

When looking at a mountain range you'll notice that all of them have peaks and valleys. The valleys are the low areas between individual mountains which separates them. Most of the vegetation resides in the valleys because when the rain comes, it collects in that area which allows for growth. The peaks are the highest points. When comparing a mountain range to our lives the valleys would be considered our low spots or times where we struggle. The peaks are the high points where accomplishment and success reside.

While we can still learn during the high times of our lives, we tend to glean more from the difficult times. These are trials in our lives. Asking God for wisdom during these trials is something I have learned to do over the years. I always want to stay in communion with Him and learn why I am going through a situation even though it was difficult. I want God's best for me and to live within His will because I know how much it will bless myself and others in the long run.

"Consider it pure joy, my brothers and sisters, whenever you face trials of many kinds, because you know that the testing of your faith produces perseverance. Let perseverance finish its work so that you may be mature and complete, not lacking anything."
James 1:2-4 (NIV)

85

In 2020 many of us were put through a trial that rocked us to our core. Some took major pay cuts, others lost jobs, and some businesses got decimated due to mandatory shutdowns. We were faced with an uphill battle to move forward with our lives, and from the ground level view the task seemed daunting or almost impossible. It's like the first step in a long hike up a mountain that's three miles high and all you are thinking about is how there is no way you will be able to make it to the summit. I'm here to tell you that you can't do it alone, because I have tried and failed. You need to put your faith in Christ to help you get there.

Failure is not something any of us look forward to. As a man I take pride in setting out to provide the best I can for my family. I hunt, I gather, I bring it home for the family. It sounds primitive, but for many of us that is our mindset. Our job is to provide, and we expect to do it well. Many of us appreciate respect more than love, and if we do a poor job of providing, we feel like we may lose our family's respect and look like a failure. What happened to me in September of 2019 was the beginning of the longest journey in the wilderness that I have ever experienced in my life, and for a while I felt so alone.

A TEST OF MY FAITH

After the 2018 season our General Manager Bobby Evans was let go by the San Francisco Giants. Bobby was a great leader and good friend and I felt so bad for him. He loved the team deeply and spent 26 years serving them. Things changed in many ways in our organization after this move and for me, I lost one of my biggest supporters. Bobby saw my leadership ability and in 2018 put me in a position with the organization to start cultivating that gift more.

I managed the Arizona Rookie Team and oversaw Extended Spring Training in 2018. This put me in a management role for the first time and I did a good job. The team was successful, the players got better, and we finished with the second-best minor league record in the organization. I was looking forward to managing again in 2019 and building off what I learned. There were definitely areas where I could improve, and I was ready to be an even better manager that next season.

Before the team named our next General Manager many, if not all the coaches, were offered contracts for the next season. I didn't know what level I would be at or what my job title might be, but I was offered a one-year deal with a slight salary bump and was encouraged to sign it as soon as possible. Later that fall, I was told that I would no longer be managing, but I would stay in Arizona as a development coach who would focus on team defense, base running, and was the first base coach.

I was disappointed at first but decided to make the best of it and focus on helping the players and coaches any way I could. As the season started something was happening between the manager of the team and myself. It seemed like everything I did wasn't good enough and he went out of his way to find fault in things I did. Other coaches and our players noticed it, but I figured things would work out. The manager and I had a few discussions, some heated, and I felt like we cleared the air, but it just got worse. He sometimes ridiculed me in front of our team, and even though it was addressed by upper management, things did not get better.

For the first time in my life, I was looking forward to the season being over. Pride started to rise up inside me and I wanted to blow up on my manager, but I stayed quiet. Aside from all my personal turmoil our team was playing outstanding. We set the record for the most wins in Arizona Rookie League history and winning the championship seemed like an afterthought. I just wanted to win, go home, and move on to a better situation next year. We didn't perform well in the playoffs and lost in the semi-finals. The season ended, I finished my game report and went home. What I didn't know was that was my last game with the Giants.

Our Farm Director called me a couple of weeks later and said that the organization would not be renewing my contract for 2020.

My current contract was guaranteed through the rest of the year, but after that I was off the payroll. I waited for a couple of days to let this set in and then began my job search. In a way I was looking forward to a fresh start. I felt like with my contacts in the game, as well as my coaching experience, it wasn't a matter of who I was going to be coaching with in 2020, but how many offers I would receive. Boy was I wrong.

October rolled into November without very many interviews. I spoke with a few teams over the phone, but nothing happened. In December my mom's health took a turn for the worse and I had to decide if I was going to travel to San Diego for the annual Baseball Winter Meetings to meet with teams. Every MLB team would be in attendance and a lot of interviews and decisions were made over this four-day span. I made the decision to stay home and on Wednesday of that week my mom and I had our final conversation face to face. She passed away on Saturday morning and I was devastated.

Pat Horton was my biggest cheerleader. When I played, she attended every game she possibly could and loved every second of them. I think that watching me play was one of her greatest joys. She was notorious for snapping photos the entire time and giving me a fist in the air to encourage me. When I became a coach, she attended those games as well, even when her health started to deteriorate. She loved baseball and she loved me even more. Heaven gained an angel that December morning and I lost one of my best friends.

Mom and I in 1986

As the calendar turned to 2020, I was without a job. Even though I had started to put more effort to resurrect Cactus, we were seeing lower attendance at our camps and clinics than we expected. I was certain that an MLB team was still going to sign me at the last minute, but everyone who seemed to be getting jobs were younger and had experience with baseball technology and analytics. When I was with the Giants, we didn't spend a lot of time or money in these areas, and I had no experience with them. The game was changing, and I was getting left behind.

Spring Training began in February, and I was in disbelief that I wasn't with a team. I was frustrated and confused with God's plan for my life. Why the heck was I not in pro baseball? What did I do wrong? Why are you allowing this to happen to me? All of these things ran through my head, and I was very discouraged. I realized I needed to put all of my efforts into Cactus because I wasn't going to be coaching in the minor leagues this year. Little did I know that no one else was either.

In March the United States of America was put on pause when the coronavirus disease shut down our country and the rest of the world. All the sudden it wasn't about missing going to the ballpark every day. It was missing out on going anywhere any day. Our kids were home from school and my wife's job now transitioned to zoom calls and emails. I could no longer do baseball lessons, camps, or clinics. My job as a substitute teacher at my son's private school was now gone, and the only income I had was from my adjunct professor position at Grand Canyon University and like everyone else, we did zoom calls.

Now I wasn't alone. So many people were out of work and all my former co-workers were just like me, not coaching baseball. It didn't make me feel any better and I didn't take pleasure in their misfortune. Thankfully for most of them they still received their full salary so they could provide for their families. I didn't have that luxury, so I had to figure out what the heck I was going to do. I was starting to get nervous about how I was going to support my family.

I was too proud to go on unemployment and once the Covid-19 restrictions started to loosen up in Arizona, I looked for work anywhere I could. A friend told me he was doing Uber Eats so I started to drive for them as well. The money was decent, but I was gone all afternoon and every night. The boys were getting restless being in the house and in the backyard by themselves and it took a toll on Taleen. She encouraged me to stop driving after a couple of months, so I bit the bullet and went on unemployment for a short time. I was embarrassed and felt more defeated than ever.

I had so much time on my hands now that I started to try and figure out how to improve myself. I decided to go online and spend the money to get certified by several different baseball technology companies. Many of the people who got jobs in the 2019 offseason had this knowledge and I wanted to match them. I also took an online Sabermetrics course and got certified in Rapsodo and K-Motion baseball technologies. I found myself really enjoying the classes and I had a new appreciation for the way baseball technology was being used in player development.

As June rolled around the Arizona Collegiate Wood Bat League was able to salvage its season and I was asked to coach one of the teams. This was awesome because I was back on the field coaching players and things started to feel a little bit normal. We played about 30 games that summer, so with the salary they paid me and the few baseball lessons I was able to do, I was able to drop unemployment before the season started. It felt great to work again, especially in an area that I loved.

As the fall approached, I planned on reaching out to teams again in the hopes they would re-consider hiring me with my newfound technology certifications. I figured that I already had the coaching experience that other people didn't have and now I had some of the knowledge they did. Plus, I have always been great in building relationships with players, so I felt like I was a slam dunk candidate for jobs. However, what I didn't think about was the fact that the people who got jobs for the 2020 season didn't get the opportunity to prove themselves because there was no season.

The teams who I spoke with said they were really impressed with the fact that I spent time and money improving myself, but the fact of the matter was they were either trying to find ways to keep their current staff members, or they were cutting back on coaches. In the winter of 2020 Major League Baseball decided to cut over 40 Minor League teams, which meant now there were less jobs in professional baseball. Oh...my...gosh, what else could go wrong for me.

In January of 2021 I started to reach out to professional Independent Baseball Leagues and Collegiate Wood Bat Leagues. These enterprises were looking for coaches with professional experience and paid a decent wage for the season. It wasn't anything close to what the Giants paid me, but it would get me through the summer. In March I started to receive offers from teams and after a lot of thought and prayer, eventually decided to become the manager of the Williamsport Crosscutters in the newly founded Major League Baseball Draft League. It was college players, but since MLB was involved, I felt like it was my best chance to get noticed by teams again.

I continued to teach at Grand Canyon University in the spring and did some substitute teaching at our sons' school. Cactus started to gain traction again with some clinics with local youth leagues and I was doing a lot of private and small group lessons. I was really looking forward to spending the summer in Pennsylvania and what made it even better was the fact that Taleen and the boys would be with me for most of the season. Her job at Impact Church allowed her to work remotely that summer, so she and the boys flew out once school finished in late May. I was able to coach a high level of baseball and had my family with me. Things were looking up.

The season in Williamsport went well. It had its ups and downs like most things do, but overall, the experience was great. The front office staff was a pleasure to work with and I had a good coaching staff. The travel was limited, so we didn't have a lot of long bus rides, and my family typically came to all the games. Taleen and the boys would stay in the hotel with me during road games and we rented a great little house in Williamsport for the summer. Connor was the team bat boy and did a fantastic job. He and Bryce were at the field almost every day shagging fly balls, hanging out in the bullpen, and taking batting practice with the team. I loved having them at the field with me.

The Boys and I during the National Anthem in Williamsport

During the week of the MLB All-Star game our league took a six-day break. Some of the players on the teams in our league had a good chance of getting drafted and the MLB draft took place that week. We took advantage of our time off and headed out to Point Pleasant Beach in New Jersey. Taleen grew up not too far from the area and went down there for vacations as a little girl. We stayed at a hotel that was walking distance from the ocean and spent four days at the beach.

The four of us all spent time in the water and I would say the boys and I got crushed by about 100 waves. I remember I got blindsided by a couple of them while I was paying attention to see where the boys were at, and on one occasion when trying to go under a wave I heard my neck crack. After our fourth day in the ocean, I went to bed feeling fine and then woke up in the morning to the room violently spinning like an out of control merry go round. I didn't know what was going on, so I laid in the bathtub with a bag of ice on my head and I felt like I was going to get sick.

Taleen took me to a local clinic where they figured out, I had vertigo. Whenever I would lay straight back and turn to my right, I would vomit. The doctor gave me a script for some medication and then we had to drive four hours back to Williamsport. When we got home, I couldn't lay flat, so I slept propped up in a recliner. I was miserable and somehow, I had to get myself together in the next 48 hours so I would be ready for our first game after the break. I felt like coaching in Williamsport was my chance to impress MLB teams with my coaching ability, so I needed to be on the field as soon as possible.

I only shared my condition with the team's General Manager, Assistant GM, and coaching staff. I figured if I started to not feel well at least they needed to know. I wasn't myself completely and it kind of reminded me about how I felt after getting a concussion in the past. I took it easy on my workouts in the gym but kept my on-field routine the same. I still threw batting practice and did defensive work with the players. I slowly started to feel better as time went on but didn't shake this completely for months.

The season continued after the break, and we had the most players drafted by MLB teams in our league. New players came in to replace them, but the vibe was different during the second half of the season. We ended up with a losing record, which was something I was not accustomed to. I think the last team I was on as a player or coach that lost more than they won was a summer league team when I was a teenager. Overall, it was a good experience, and the players learned a lot from our coaching staff. My family boarded the plane in August and headed back home to the desert.

In most parts of the country once the sports calendar turns to September, many young boys are playing football and baseball is only played by professionals. Not in Arizona. I don't love it that's for sure, but this is my opportunity to share what I know with young people. I show them how to play the game the right way at a high level and also be an example of a Christian in the way I speak and act. With Cactus we focused on small group training this time in the fall and not clinics. Those would come in the spring.

I started to reach out to MLB teams once the boys went back to school. About 15 teams reached back out to me in the fall and I really felt good about a few of them. I interviewed with Cleveland multiple times, and they even flew me out for a final interview at Progressive Field. I felt like I didn't completely nail the final interview but was positive about my chances to land a job with them. They called me around 5pm the day before Thanksgiving to let me know that... I didn't get the position.

Taleen's family was in town, and they were all in the kitchen having fun preparing some of the dishes for the next day. I was in our office at home when I received the news, and I called her in to let her know. Saying she was disappointed would be an understatement. I was a little numb and started to wonder if I was ever going to work in professional baseball again. My favorite time of the year runs from the week of Thanksgiving through New Year's Day and in 2021 it was off to a terrible start.

I continued to talk to MLB teams over the next couple months, but no interviews materialized. I got to the point where I was very discouraged and then something hit. In February the Milwaukee Brewers had an opening for a minor league hitting coach and I started the interview process with them. It was going great and within a couple weeks I was a finalist for the job. After my final interview I felt very confident that I was going to get hired. I received the call from someone in their front office a couple days later and what he told me literally knocked the wind out of me. I didn't get the job.

A week later Spring Training started and now I started focusing on opportunities with Independent and College Wood Bat League teams again. I was offered a hitting coach position with an Indy Ball team in New York and strongly considered it. I also was offered the opportunity to be the Field Coordinator for the Arizona Collegiate Wood Bat League. The Indy Ball job was more money, but I would be gone from home for four months. Ultimately Taleen and I decided that staying home for less money was the better option.

Our clinics and private training with Cactus were starting to flourish again, and I spent a lot of time helping individual youth teams by helping run their practices. I was teaching the coaches as much as the kids and let me tell you spending an hour with a bunch of 6-year-olds at a t-ball practice will test the patience of any man! However, I really enjoyed spending time with all of the teams, and they were so appreciative. I knew I was making a difference and that's why God had me start Cactus in the first place.

My competitive nature and the fact that I was making quite a bit less staying in Arizona was tough to swallow, but it was the best decision. There were 21 teams in the league, and my job was to make sure everything ran smoothly. This had more of a front office type feel and I didn't coach any of the teams. Connor ran the concession stand and he learned how to drive a golf cart. Our bond got even stronger that summer. Bryce doesn't love watching baseball, so he stayed home most days, but we still hung out during the mornings and early afternoons.

The season ended in late July, and we took a family trip to Mexico before school started. In late August I began to call MLB teams again hoping that my newest experience over the summer would enhance my resume and improve my chances for a job. I had some good conversations with teams and interviewed for minor league manager positions with the Oakland A's, Pittsburgh Pirates and Boston Red Sox. I felt like I crushed every interview, but yet again I didn't get a job offer. What the heck do I need to do to get a job?!!

As the fall turned to winter, I was still talking to some MLB teams, but it felt like they were in no rush to fill their positions. I had a major sense of urgency to find a job and I was done waiting around. I began to contact Independent League teams again, and in January an opportunity presented itself in the Pioneer League. It was a manager position, and the owner said the roster was barren and I had full autonomy to build it as I saw fit. This was very intriguing.

****

Setbacks in our lives are not fun and none of us look forward to them. The situation you find yourself in sometimes doesn't make sense and may seem unfair. You're trying the best you can, and your heart is in the right place, but things are just not working out. When this happens it's important to remember that you can only control the controllables in life. Things like effort, attitude, and work ethic are qualities to focus on. Doing this will allow you to have freedom and peace of mind during the setback, and let God do His work while He prunes and grows you during this time.

"Every branch in Me that does not bear fruit, He takes away; and every branch that bears fruit, He prunes it so that it may bear more fruit."
John 15:2 (NASB)

LIFE APPLICATION

1. Put life into perspective when times get tough.
2. Prioritize things and make the most important ones first.
3. Learn to focus on what you can control and let go of what you can't.
4. Gain wisdom from past experiences and apply them to your current situation.
5. Focus on the lesson God is teaching you instead of the problems you are facing.

NOTES:

STUDY QUESTIONS

1. What did you learn about yourself during your last setback?
2. What steps did you take to turn the situation around?
3. How can you prepare yourself better the next time you enter into the wilderness?

NOTES:

THE COMEBACK

Applying the TODAY Mentality

In my eight years with the San Francisco Giants, we accomplished a lot. In 2012, we defeated my home-town team, the Detroit Tigers, in the World Series. We followed that up in 2014 with another World Series Championship when we beat the Kansas City Royals in a heart stopping seven games. Both championships netted me a World Series ring and the players on the team voted to divide up a playoff share and distribute it amongst the minor league coaches. What a huge financial blessing that was for a family saving up to buy a home.

On the minor league side, I spent all eight years in the Arizona Rookie League. This kept me home with my family and allowed me to run Cactus during our peak years as a business. Connor and Bryce would come to the field with me and attended as many games as they could. Our winning percentage over that time was .612 and we went to the playoffs in four of those years. We competed three times in the league championship series and won it in 2013. When I left the Giants after the 2019 season, over twenty of our minor league players made their Major League debut in the big leagues.

Let's wind back the clock a little further. During my time working for the Arizona Diamondbacks (2001-2003, 2006) we won the World Series in 2001. Back when I played minor league baseball, I was on the Northeast League Champion New Jersey Jackals in 1998. As a collegiate athlete at Spring Hill College our winning percentage from 1992-1995 was .667, the highest four-year span for any SHC baseball team in school history. Every team I played for at Cactus High School had winning records except one that went .500.

Why am I telling you all of this? Because at some point I had to tell myself that you're not a loser. Even though you keep being told that you're not good enough, your track record shows that you are. As much as I would pump up other people's tires and encourage them during tough times, I felt like a failure. I wasn't providing for my family the way I wanted to. All the "NO's" started to pile up and my mind went to a very dark and desperate place. The devil had me where he wanted me- wounded and feeling all alone. He wanted to take me down, but I have something that he doesn't. A best friend named JESUS!

PIVOTING BACK TO PRO BASEBALL

As the calendar turned to 2023, I was still talking with the Boston Red Sox and Toronto Blue Jays about coaching positions, but things were moving slower than molasses in January. Considering it was January was coincidental, but I didn't find that as funny as I normally would. Then something finally happened that gave me some hope. On January 14th I received a phone call from the owner of the Billings Mustangs. Our interview lasted less than an hour and when I got off the phone, I felt very good about my chances of landing this job.

This wasn't the first time the owner and I had spoken. I interviewed for the same managing position in January of 2022, but it went to another candidate. He had Major League management experience, so I fully understood why he was chosen. He only stayed for one season, so once I found out it was open, I reached out to Billing's General Manager in October of 2022. We spoke a few times through the fall, but nothing materialized until the owner called on January 14th. Two days later he offered me the job and I accepted. Now the hard work really started.

The roster was completely barren. We had zero players and no coaches. At this point most Independent League teams have at least half of their roster signed, and I was in foreign territory. I had never recruited players in the past and now I had to sign at least 30 of them over the next 3 months. I started calling every scout and coach I knew, especially the coaches who had ties to Indy ball. I found out about a month-long winter baseball league in Palm Springs, CA that started in late January, so with Taleen's blessing I got in my truck and headed out to my first scouting event.

My sister Sharon lives in Palm Springs, so I stayed with her. The league had over 200 players, so my mind was spinning from the outset. I was only going to be there for four days, so I had to pinpoint players I liked quickly and focus on them. In addition to scouting, I also made a lot of great relationships with other managers and coaches who were there as well. This helped during the season when I called them about potential trades. I left with a new appreciation for what scouts go through and within a month we signed four players out of that league. This started to become the foundation of our team.

When I got back home, I needed to focus on another big event for Cactus that had been in the works for months. We were partnering again with ELI Marketing for another fantasy camp with the ESPN executives and their families during Super Bowl LVII in Glendale, AZ. We used the Spring Training facility for the Chicago White Sox and Los Angeles Dodgers again, and this time we did a Little League baseball theme. ELI was paying us more than they did in the past, so this was big for Cactus because we were not going to run summer camps in 2023. Our coaches did a great job and just like the last two times we worked for ELI the results were outstanding.

As the spring started to transition to summer our Billings roster grew, and I felt good about the players we had coming in for our spring training in mid-May. However, only one week before I left for Montana something happened. Eight of our players were unable to make it to spring training. Three of them had visa or work permit issues, four of them got injured, and one more decided to retire. What the heck?! We just went from 32 players to 24, and it took us a very long time to get to 32! I had to go back and hit the phones and literally we were signing players during my three-day drive north to Billings.

We ended up signing seven more players within a week and started our spring training. Montana is a beautiful state and the stadium we played in was outstanding. We started the season out in solid fashion going 3-3 in our first six games versus the best team in the league. Things were looking good and then the skid happened- we lost nine games in a row. The Billings Mustangs were celebrating their 75th year as a professional baseball team and we just tied their longest losing streak in franchise history. Not good.

Some people in the front office got a little flustered, but our team stood strong. One thing I do not discuss is winning and losing. In my opinion John Wooden is the greatest coach in sports history. He didn't discuss winning and the teams he coached at UCLA won ten National Championships. TEN! That's good enough for me. One of our mantras was "One in a row." That didn't matter if it was a winning streak or losing streak. It was always one game in a row. This saying would pay off later in the season.

We ended up playing better over the next month and as we entered the start of July, we were only two games under .500. Things were looking up, but then we hit another bad streak, and we lost ten of our next twelve games. At the same time two of our best players got picked up by the Los Angeles Angels and Arizona Diamondbacks. It was now the halfway point of the season, and we were ten games under .500. The team was playing without a lot of energy, and we looked listless in my eyes. We were being outplayed, outcoached, and worst of all outhustled. I was angry and changes needed to be made. Very difficult changes.

We traded one of our most popular players and released a few more. Our locker room needed an identity change. We added some hungry players who were fast, hit for power, and pitchers who threw strikes. They were passed over in the recent Major League Draft and they had something to prove. So, did I. That made us a perfect match. I went to my coaches and told them I needed to do a better job and so did they. We started to scout other teams with the data we had, and the wins started to slowly pile up. Then in late July something terrible happened.

Our son Bryce sustained a knee injury, and it required surgery. Taleen and the boys had to leave Montana early and to say the least it hit all of us hard. Bryce has been blessed with God given speed and strength and now he was entering the most difficult challenge of his life. He would be on crutches for the next several months and unable to play sports for his entire 7th grade year. Taleen was devastated and her workload went through the roof. Now she was balancing a full-time job and taking care of both boys without me. To say she was stressed was an understatement. I felt helpless being 1,000 miles away and my heart was not in the game. I felt bad for her, and I missed my family.

My Family on the Field in Billings

It was mid-August, and I asked our front office for permission to fly home for a few days to spend time with my family. I didn't tell anyone back home I was coming except our next-door neighbor Jackie who was going to pick me up at the airport. I informed the team after our game on Saturday, August 19th that I was leaving early the next morning, and I would miss the game on Sunday. We had an off day on Monday, and I would be back for the game on Tuesday. We lost the game on the 19th, but it would be the last time that happened for a long, long, time.

I walked in the front door of our house and Taleen started crying. The boys were in disbelief and our dog Rusty went nuts. I was only home for 48 hours, but it felt like a week to Taleen. It gave her a boost of energy and lifted her spirits. I sat on the couch and hugged Bryce, and we talked about how cool his scar was. I didn't check the score of our game and had no plans to until my phone rang telling me a fight almost broke out because someone got hit by a pitch. I've been gone for like twelve hours and now this happens?! It turned out things got blown way out of proportion and our coaches took care of everything. No big deal. Problem solved. Please let me focus on my family.

The team won 5-0 on Sunday, and on Tuesday morning I flew back to Montana. Everyone asked about how Bryce was doing which I really appreciated. I missed my family, but it was good to get back to work. Something felt different. I was at peace with what was going on and I left everything in God's hands. It was out of my control anyway, so I just focused on our team. We had been playing better over the past three weeks and the locker room was confident. We won the night I got back and continued to do so for almost three more weeks.

We won fifteen games in a row and went 17-2 down the stretch. During the winning streak I was getting interview requests and every time I had the chance, I gave God all the glory and the players all the credit. I paraphrased Psalm 143:10 to one reporter, and he went out of his way to find the complete verse and put it in the article. When I read that article, I closed my office door at the

106

ballpark, got on my knees, and wept. God was doing something amazing, and I could feel His presence. I was in awe of what was happening, and I was overcome with emotion.

> *"Teach me to do your will, for you are my God;*
> *may your good Spirit lead me on level ground."*
> **Psalm 143:10 (NIV)**

We qualified for the playoffs on the last day of the season in a crazy game on the road in Colorado when the opposing team had the tying and winning runs on base in the bottom of the 9th inning. I cried on the field after that win and the pressure of the season left me at that moment. It was replaced with a peace that can only be described one that comes from God. We ended up playing Missoula in the first round of the playoffs. They had the best overall record in the league, but we played well against them all year. We won that series, and the final game was as crazy as our season. A 12-inning road win in front of a hostile crowd. Absolutely amazing. No tears after this one. Just joy.

The championship series was next, and we headed out to Ogden, UT with a lot of confidence. Overall, we played well, but didn't capitalize on some opportunities we had. Ogden was the better team that series and I tip my cap to them. Their manager Kash Beauchamp is a friend, so I was happy for him. What's crazy is that Kash was my manager back in 1998 when we won a championship together with the New Jersey Jackals. We had a team meeting after the final game, and I told the players I loved them and how proud I was of our season. The next day I was on the road headed back to Arizona and I was excited to see my family again.

A week later I spoke with our owner, and he didn't offer me a contract for 2024. I was a bit surprised, and a large part of me thought it came down to money. I was the lowest paid manager in the league, and in the coming weeks I would be named the 2023 Pioneer League Manager of the Year. I deserved more. I told our

General Manager at the end of the season that I was willing to take the league's average salary for managers, but we didn't even get to a place of negotiations. They decided to move on to someone else.

Multiple opportunities were presented to me within days and after a lot of thought and prayer I decided to take a risk and accept an offer to manage a new Pioneer League expansion team in Northern California near Sacramento. The team didn't have a name, a stadium, and no front office personnel. I was literally their first employee. I believed in the vision that the owners cast and look the plunge. They also named me the Assistant General Manager in charge of Player Procurement. I went from being the lowest paid manager in the league to one of the highest, and the salary was more than what the Giants used to pay me. Amazing how God works.

It was early October, and I was not going to mess around. Billings hired me in mid-January. Now I had a four-month head start in the recruiting process and I got to work. From October through April, I had phone interviews with at least 100 players and attended five scouting events across the country where I saw over 500 players. We signed 33 of them. Countless others contacted me directly or through their agents, but I didn't have in-depth conversations with all of them. I asked a lot of leading questions and wanted to get to know these young men as best as I could. I wanted to make sure that they represented our team well and that I wanted to spend four months of my life with them.

Wise leaders surround themselves with people who have different gifts and the same vision, so hiring the right people for my coaching staff was a big priority. The only staff member who followed me from Billings was our head of scouting and analytics, AJ Crapo. He is trustworthy, did a great job, and I've known him for ten years. Next, I hired Gary Davenport as our bench coach. We worked together for eight years with the Giants, and I always appreciated his knowledge and love of the game. Jerome Williams came highly recommended by a manager in the MLB Draft League, and he agreed to be our pitching coach. His work ethic and ability to communicate with players made him my number one target to lead our pitching staff.

Cactus centered its focus on local youth baseball leagues in the spring and I also did private lessons. Because I would be gone again for a second straight summer, I felt like going back to running summer camps was not in our best interest yet. I did continue to volunteer as a baseball coach at our son's school, and to my pleasant surprise many of the varsity high school baseball players had attended our camps and played in our winter league when they were younger. It was cool to see how they had grown as players as well as young men. Hearing their stories about how much they loved playing in the AZBL brought a huge smile to my face and warmed my heart.

Our Spring Training started on May 13th and there was excitement in the air. Our coaches knew we had a talented club, and it was going to be tough to whittle down our roster to 26 players. On top of them being talented, they were also great young men. Releasing any of them was going to be hard. We had a great first practice and then played games the next five days in a row. The first three games we had practices in the mornings and intersquad games in the afternoons. We played the Oakland Ballers the next two games and didn't perform great, but I really liked our team's athleticism. We made our roster cuts and had two more light practices to complete spring training.

It's hard to put into words, but there is something so electric about opening day in baseball. It's a special day and even typing these words brings a smile to my face now. We opened the season at home versus the Rocky Mountain Vibes on May 21st and held a 4-3 lead going into the top of the 6th inning. We had come back from a 3-0 deficit and were feeling really good. Then the manager from the Vibes walked out to home plate to have a discussion with the umpire. I was called over to be a part of it and that's when our season changed dramatically.

The stadium we played at in Davis did not have permanent lights, so during the offseason our owners planned on using temporary lights as a solution. The delivery was postponed, and the lights went up at the last minute. They were tested the night before opening day and our front office felt like they were going be fine for the season. When we turned them on in the 5th inning, we could tell we had issues. They were not tall enough and the lights blinded the infielders. It was also dim in spots in the outfield. We tried to adjust the lights over the next week, but nothing worked. We now had to come to the realization that all our home games would be in the daytime.

Our home games were hot, but it allowed our team to test a phrase I gave them in spring training about overcoming adversity, "The hotter it is, the better we play!" This phrase applied to all weather conditions and on a given day when I would say the first part, the team would emphatically yell out the second part. We also had to deal with other daily inconveniences like the twenty-minute walk from the team clubhouse to the field, paying for parking, inconsistent weight room times, a new trainer every week, and a lack of pre-game food. The guys started to get frustrated so after communicating this to our ownership the food budget was increased. The other things were out of our control.

The blessing out of all this chaos was the players banding together like brothers. They took on the moniker of "Team 12" which was what some people called us prior to our team being officially announced in late January as the 12th team in the Pioneer League. The owners of our team also owned the other Pioneer League expansion team in Oakland. This team was announced two months prior to us, and it was very apparent that our owners spent more time and effort with the Oakland team both in the off-season and during the season.

Our owners marketed Oakland way more and invested significantly more time in that community. I understand it from a financial standpoint because they could make more money with Oakland. Our team was drawing minimal fans, and they were taking huge losses to keep us afloat. Our players didn't see that. They just saw owners who attended our games when we played in Oakland but didn't come to our home games. It pissed the players off and all our guys wanted to do was prove to our owners that we were the better team.

We played good in the first half of the season, but we got stuck in neutral most of the time. We win a few in a row, then lose a few. Our team was young compared to some of the other teams in the league and we made too many fundamental mistakes. It was frustrating because I could see our potential, but we weren't executing consistently like great teams do. However, the silver lining was the guys loved playing together and they were getting better. I told our coaches that I would be content if we were at .500 at the break because I felt like we could make a run in the second half. When the first half ended, we were 23-23 and had just won seven of our last ten games. Things were looking up.

The second half began on July 16th, and we won three games in a row. Things looked great and then we went on a crazy 21 game road trip over the next 24 days which is unheard of in professional baseball. During the first week of the trip, we started to sputter and had a team meeting. I asked the guys if they thought they were a great team. They said yes. I asked them if they thought it was achievable to go 11-10 on this road trip, and they more emphatically said, YES! All we had to do was win one more than we lost and if that happened, we would be four games over .500 and in a spot to compete for the playoffs.

The plan was laid out, and the guys were on board. We didn't play great the next week but played outstanding the final week of the trip and lo and behold our record that road trip was exactly 11-10. We went home confident and knew we had a tough task against the first-place team in the league, Boise. Once we were back home, we flipped a switch. We battered Boise over the next two weeks beating them ten out of the next twelve games, with the final six games being at their place. We came back home with the opportunity to clinch a playoff spot and the team standing in our way was…. Oakland.

Our magic number to get into the playoffs was two that final week. Oakland's was three. How crazy is it that both expansion teams, owned by the same people, had a chance to make the playoffs. Home field advantage in the playoffs was also on the line. The series went back and forth, and we each won three games. We clinched our playoff spot first, but Oakland ended up with home field advantage in the playoffs. Missoula was the one seed, Oakland was the two, we were the three seed, and Glacier was the four. We were now set to play Oakland in a best of three series and Game 1 was set to be in Davis just two days after the season ended. Our players were foaming at the mouth.

We smacked Oakland in Game 1, 14 to 4 and headed to their park for Game 2. We did not like it there at all. Our locker room was a converted public restroom, their ballpark was in a bad area, and the fans were loud and obnoxious. It had that Yankees-Red Sox feel on a smaller level. They beat us 1-0 in Game 2, which set up winner take all Game 3 in Oakland. Their players showed up that day during batting practice donned in playoff t-shirts, yet we didn't have any. Same owners, different treatment. One of our pitchers made a very funny comment that I won't repeat, and we went into that game focused.

Game 3 had everything you wanted to decide a series. We scored early and Oakland fought back. The game was 4-3 after 6 innings and we got on the board again in the 7th with 2 more runs. Oakland responded with a run of their own in the bottom of the frame, but those were the last runs scored. A fly ball to centerfield in the bottom of the 9th ended the game and we jumped up and down like little kids near the mound. We went out to the bullpen to celebrate more with champaign baths and coolers getting dumped on coaches. We beat them on their field, and we did it for us.

We moved on to the best of five Championship Series versus Glacier. Now we had the home field advantage, and the first two games were up in Kalispell, Montana. They have a beautiful field and I love playing in Montana, so I was excited to get up there. All the players were motivated, but a handful of them maybe more than others. Last year the Billings team I managed lost in the Championship and four players on our current Yolo roster were on that team. We had unfinished business and we planned on taking care of it.

The first two games of the series were highlighted by pitching and defense. We lost Game 1, by a score of 2-0 and then won Game 2 by the narrowest of margins 2-1. We headed back home for Game 3 with a lot of confidence. We were back in sunny California and one thing we joked about is that our team was solar powered. We played great during the daytime. Game 3 was another close one and after the first 4 innings we were tied 2-2. We pulled away with 3 runs in the 5th and won 6-4. We were one win away from wrapping up the title.

Bobby Lada was our primary second baseman during the season. He's a quiet player who has a lot of faith and a ton of tools. He came up big in Game 2 with an RBI single in the 8th inning and before that at-bat we had a quick conversation about honoring the Lord with his play. During batting practice before Game 3 someone in our dugout congratulated him on the big hit and he said, "I've been talking with Billy, and I just wanted to honor the Lord with that at bat". I happened to be walking by when he said that, and I realized how God was working within our team. We had 15-20 people each week attending chapel and I felt His presence so many times on the field.

Game 4 started out rough. We were down 5-0 early and we couldn't seem to get going. Then in the 6th inning Bobby hit a solo home run and the next 3 guys got on base. That set the stage for Tanner Smith, and he tied the game with a grand slam. The very next inning Glacier scored 2 more which was a gut punch, but we had been here before and overcame much bigger deficits. We were

113

still down two runs going into the bottom of the 9th and that's when things got crazy. With two outs and runners on first and second, Bobby walked to the plate. I pointed to the sky. He did the same and tapped his heart. On the first pitch he saw, he hit a towering fly ball down the left field line. It was starting to hook and then…..it hit the top of the foul pole. It was a 3 run WALK OFF HOMER!!!

Bedlam ensued. Bobby threw his bat above where our lights were supposed to be, and everyone poured out of the dugout. I was jumping up and down and yelling in the 3rd base coaches box. The team ripped off Bobby's jersey at home plate and tears welled up as I hugged that kid as hard as I could. I walked out to center field, hit my knees, lifted my hands in the air and cried tears of joy. What in the world did you just do God?! I walked back towards home plate, had a few conversations, and before I could get to our dugout, I broke down in tears again. God was there and I was in awe of His presence.

We popped champaign bottles again and this time it was on our field. Our players and staff overcame so much adversity during the season and that made this celebration even more satisfying. The players, coaches, and front office all hung out that night together at dinner and we recalled fun stories from the season around a firepit. I traveled home a couple days later to a very happy household and in early October I was once again named the Pioneer League Manager of the Year. As always, God's plan for my life was better than mine.

2024 Pioneer League Champion Yolo High Wheelers

Cactus is still impacting the Phoenix community in a positive way through our clinics and events. The business is not a big as it was in its heyday, but we are still teaching kids the game of baseball and life lessons along the way. My passion to be a great influence in children's lives is still there, but I feel like God has been moving me more towards young men in recent years. Being an example of Christ both on and off the field to the players I am coaching now at the minor league level is my mission field. I believe God has me right where He wants me, and I'll continue to do His work wherever I'm placed by Him.

Everyone likes a good comeback story. However, you can't have one unless there is a setback that happens before it. When I was growing up, I rooted a lot for the underdog. You know, the person or team that people overlooked and didn't expect much from. Throughout my life I had people doubt that I would amount to much in baseball. For a long time, their doubt fueled my fire, but eventually I realized that trying to prove them wrong was wasted energy. Honoring God with the gifts that He blessed me with and glorifying Him in my everyday life is more important. Success is not what the scoreboard says at the end of the game or what your net worth is. Success is defined as preparing and working the best you can and being content with the result in the end. Trusting God with your future is one of the best decisions you will ever make in life, and I encourage you to do it **TODAY**.

"Each of you has been blessed with one of God's many wonderful gifts to be used in the service of others. So use your gift well."
1 Peter 4:10 (CEV)

LIFE APPLICATION

1. Believe in yourself and stay humble.
2. Focus on being the best version of you, instead of comparing yourself to others.
3. Write down attainable and lofty goals and focus on how to accomplish them.
4. Regardless of the number of doubters, remember that God plus you is the majority.
5. As long as you believe you are within God's will for your life, keep fighting!

NOTES:

_____

_____

_____

_____

_____

_____

_____

_____

_____

_____

STUDY QUESTIONS

1. When your comeback happens what can you do to maintain your success?
2. With your newfound success what will you do with your new platform?
3. What are some ways you can honor God with the success you've achieved?

NOTES:

EPILOGUE

The 2024 season was the most fun I ever had as a coach. I feel I also made the most impact on people for Christ during the season. More than any other year in my life, God used me to impact others through the game of baseball. His love for everyone is the message. Baseball is the vehicle to deliver that message. I am humbled that He is using me the way He is, but that's the whole point of this book. When you are in line with God's plan for your life, He will use you in ways you could only dream of and the joy you will feel is something you will cherish forever.

For your dream to come to fruition you need to step out in faith and take a step forward towards starting the process. A journey always begins with one step. Too many people allow their dream to die due to the fear of the unknown. Yes, the odds may be stacked against you but who cares? I would rather give my best effort and fall short, than to wonder what I could have done. The following quote by Nathan Whitley is one of my new favorites. "The pain of regret is far worse than the pain of discipline."

I have slept in my car, on stranger's couches, and on top of a freaking dugout, all just to play the game I loved. I was willing to do almost anything to realize my dream and there were plenty of obstacles and doubters along the way. It was all just noise and eventually I learned to block it out. When you are within God's will for your life there is no promise that the road will be easy. The question you need ask yourself is are you willing to step out of the boat and be willing to get wet?

Be fierce. Take chances. Blaze your own trail and enjoy the scenery along the way. Exhaust all your efforts and have zero regrets. You have been given one life to live on this Earth and I want every one of you to reach your full potential. God created you to be great. He has amazing plans for you and has planted seeds of your dreams in your heart. I believe you will always be more successful when you are passionate about what you do. I know I am.

"I have fought the good fight, I have finished the race, I have kept the faith."
2 Timothy 4:7 (ESV)

GLOSSARY OF VERSES

TAKE ACTION

- *"Now faith is confidence in what we hope for and assurance about what we do not see."*
  - Hebrews 11:1 (NIV)

- *"This is the confidence we have in approaching God: that if we ask anything according to his will, he hears us."*
  - 1 John 5:14 (NIV)

- *"I can do all things through Christ who strengthens me."*
  - Philippians 4:13 (NKJV)

OVERCOME

- *"Immediately Jesus made the disciples get into the boat and go on ahead of Him to the other side, while He dismissed the crowds. After He had sent them away, He went up on the mountain by Himself to pray. When evening came, He was there alone, but the boat was already far from the land, buffeted by the waves because the wind was against it.*

  During the fourth watch of the night, Jesus went out to them, walking on the sea. When the disciples saw him walking on the sea, they were terrified. "It is a ghost!" they said, and cried out in fear. But Jesus spoke up at once: "Take courage! It is I. Do not be afraid." "Lord if it is You" Peter replied, "command me to come to you on the water." "Come," Jesus said.

Then Peter got down out of the boat, walked on the water, and came toward Jesus. But when he saw the strength of the wind, he was afraid, and beginning to sink, cried out, "Lord, save me!" Immediately Jesus reached out His hand and took hold of Peter. "You of little faith," He said, "why did you doubt?" And when they had climbed back into the boat, the wind died down. Then those who were in the boat worshiped Him, saying, "Truly You are the Son of God!"

- Matthew 14:22-33 (BSB)

- *"Plans fail for lack of counsel, but with many advisers they succeed."*
    - Proverbs 15:22 (NIV)

- *"This is my command—be strong and courageous! Do not be afraid or discouraged. For the LORD your God is with you wherever you go."*
    - Joshua 1:9 (NLT)

DREAM

- *"Commit your works to the LORD and your plans will be achieved."*
    - Proverbs 16:3 (BSB)

- *"Let each of you look not only to his own interests, but also to the interests of others."*
    - Philippians 2:4 (ESV)

ACHIEVE

- *"You see that his faith and his actions were working together, and his faith was made complete by what he did."*
  - James 2:22 (NIV)

- *"In all your ways acknowledge Him, And He shall direct your paths."*
  - Proverbs 3:6 (NKJV)

YES

- *"And not only that, but we also glory in tribulations, knowing that tribulation produces perseverance: and perseverance, character; and character hope."*
  - Romans 5:3,4 (NKJV)

- *"With the tongue we bless our Lord and Father, and with it we curse men, who have been made in God's likeness. Out of the same mouth come blessing and cursing. My brothers this should not be!"*
  - James 3:9,10 (BSB)

- *"And all these blessings shall come upon you and overtake you, because you obey the voice of the LORD your God."*
  - Deuteronomy 28:2 (NKJV)

THE SETBACK

- *"Consider it pure joy, my brothers and sisters, whenever you face trials of many kinds, because you know that the testing of your faith produces perseverance. Let perseverance finish its work so that you may be mature and complete, not lacking anything."*
  - James 1:2-4 (NIV)

- *"Every branch in Me that does not bear fruit, He takes away; and every branch that bears fruit, He prunes it so that it may bear more fruit."*
  - John 15:2 (NASB)

THE COMEBACK

- *"Teach me to do your will, for you are my God; may your good Spirit lead me on level ground."*
  - Psalm 143:10 (NIV)

- *"Each of you has been blessed with one of God's many wonderful gifts to be used in the service of others. So use your gift well."*
  - 1 Peter 4:10 (CEV)

EPILOGUE

- *"I have fought the good fight, I have finished the race, I have kept the faith."*
  - 2 Timothy 4:7 (ESV)

ABOUT THE AUTHOR

Billy Horton is a professional baseball coach and the Founder of Cactus Athletics. Since 2006 this organization has been providing professional baseball and exercise training for youth ages 8 to 18 years old in the greater Phoenix, AZ area. He is also the author of the book *7 Day Fast,* the poem *Playing for God,* and has written hundreds on online articles.

He has over 20 years of coaching experience and was named the 2024 Manager of the Year in the Pioneer League when he skippered the Yolo High Wheelers to the League Championship in their inaugural season. He also won the Manager of the Year award in 2023 when he led the Billings Mustangs to the North Division Championship and an appearance in the League Championship Series.

He was a Minor League Coach for the San Francisco Giants from 2012 to 2019 which includes their World Series titles in 2012 and 2014. In his 8 years as a coach with the Giants, his teams compiled a .612 winning percentage, 4 trips to the playoffs, 3 appearances in the Championship series, and won the Championship in 2013. He has also worked in different capacities for the Arizona Diamondbacks, including their World Series Championship in 2001, Chicago White Sox, and Texas Rangers.

Even though he was cut his freshman year at Cactus High School, he eventually earned a baseball scholarship to play collegiality at Spring Hill College in Mobile, Alabama. He went on to play in the Minor Leagues from 1997-2000 for multiple Independent League teams and attended Spring Training as a player with the Chicago White Sox (1999) and Los Angeles Angels (2000).

Billy lives in Scottsdale, AZ with his beautiful wife Taleen, their two incredible sons, Connor and Bryce, and Rusty his faithful canine buddy. He has been on the board of directors for multiple charitable organizations and currently serves in the men's ministry at Impact Church.

**Scan here to learn more about
Billy Horton
And his published works**

BASEBALL AND FAMILY MEMORIES

Cactus Summer Baseball Camp

Arizona Baseball League

Baseball Family Photo in 2014

Coaching with the San Francisco Giants
in the Minor Leagues

Hiking Camelback Mountain with Connor and Bryce

Backyard Races during 2020

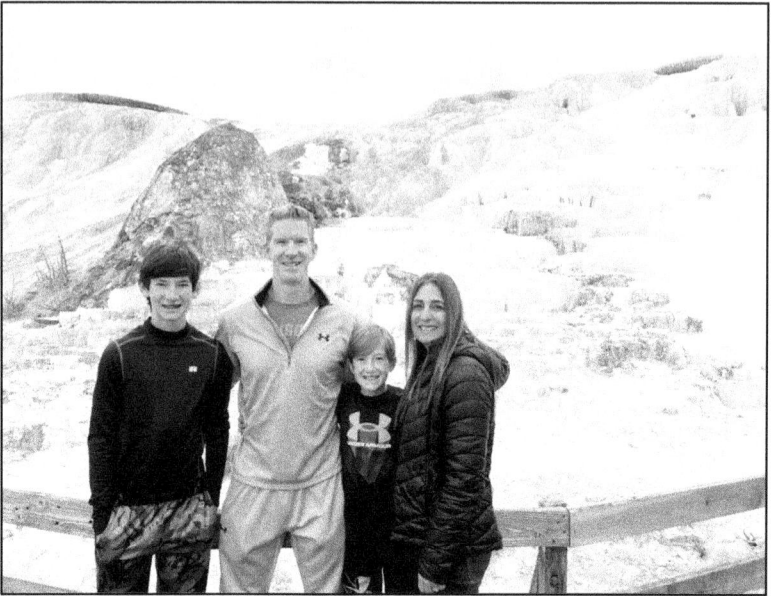

Family Trip to Yellowstone Park in 2023

Baseball Family Photo in 2024

www.ingramcontent.com/pod-product-compliance
Lightning Source LLC
LaVergne TN
LVHW051600080426
835510LV00020B/3062